Praise for *The Cost of Quiet*

"A courageous and soul-stirring guide for anyone who longs to be heard. With bold compassion and practical brilliance, Colette Jane Fehr reveals how speaking with fierce honesty doesn't create conflict, but instead sparks deeper connection and enduring intimacy."

—**Sally Hogshead**, *The New York Times* **bestselling author of** *Fascinate*

"This book is a compassionate, practical guide to having the hard conversations that truly deepen connection. It's a must-read for anyone who wants to build secure, lasting love."

—**Fran Hauser, bestselling author of** *The Myth of the Nice Girl*

"The book's central insight is revolutionary yet simple: staying quiet to 'keep the peace' actually creates the very disconnection we're trying to prevent. *The Cost of Quiet* offers hope that it's never too late to transform both your relationship with yourself and others through the power of truthful, loving communication. This is not just a book; it's a transformative journey toward personal liberation." —**Dr. Nadine Macaluso, author of** *Run Like Hell*

"When we avoid hard conversations, it doesn't just cost us emotionally; we see the fall out in our sexual lives. Fehr gives couples the language and courage to have conversations that deepen intimacy, spark desire, and create lasting sexual connections. . . . A brilliant, compassionate guide."

—**Juliana Hauser, PhD, LMFT, LPC, author of** *A New Position on Sex*

"It's normal to fear conflict and want to avoid it at all costs. But staying silent when things get tough destroys relationships. Here's the good news: You can learn to have the hard conversations with your partner that will actually save your marriage. *The Cost of Quiet* shows you *how* to speak up in your relationship—and *why* you must."

—**George Faller, MS, LMFT, author of** *True Connection*

THE
COST
OF
QUIET

How to Have the Hard
Conversations That Create Secure,
Lasting Love

Colette Jane Fehr, LMFT, LMHC

G. P. Putnam's Sons
New York

PUTNAM
— EST. 1838 —

G. P. Putnam's Sons
Publishers Since 1838
An imprint of Penguin Random House LLC
1745 Broadway, New York, NY 10019
penguinrandomhouse.com

Book design by Silverglass Studio

Library of Congress Cataloging-in-Publication Data has been applied for.

Hardcover ISBN: 9780593852743
eBook ISBN: 9780593852750

Printed in the United States of America
1st Printing

The authorized representative in the EU for product safety and compliance is Penguin
Random House Ireland, Morrison Chambers, 32 Nassau Street, Dublin D02 YH68,
Ireland, https://eu-contact.penguin.ie.

For my beloved daughters, Charlotte and Curran—
may you never let your voice be silenced.

Contents

CONTENTS

Conflict Avoidance: The Silent Killer of Relationships

"I wish I had spoken up sooner," my client Anna said, shaking her head.

She and her husband of thirty-five years had just filed for divorce. Actually, to be clear, Anna had filed for divorce—after years of feeling overlooked, underappreciated, and misunderstood. Now their kids had moved out, they were nearing retirement, and Anna was fed up with the status quo. Still, before moving forward with the proceedings, *something* brought them to my couch. It was one last-ditch effort to see if their relationship could be saved.

"I'm shocked you want to go through with this, Anna," said her husband, John. "I had no idea things were this bad."

"The truth is, I didn't know how to voice my feelings." Anna turned to me. "It never seemed to go well when I tried, so I gave up. Now I'm so bitter and resentful, I don't know if I could feel differently about him even if I wanted to."

I hear stories like this all the time. As a licensed marriage and family therapist (LMFT) and licensed mental health counselor (LMHC), I've helped hundreds of couples who desperately want to connect—or, at least, they once did, before things got so broken. Now they've been quiet for so long that they can no longer find the words to speak up.

One of the most common myths about couples therapy is that it's where relationships go to die. People assume that partners come in hissing like feral cats, sparring across the couch, and sputtering their last contentious breaths behind closed doors and sound machines. While there are some couples like this—"high-conflict couples," as we call them in the therapy world—the truth is that the counseling room is usually far quieter than you might imagine. That's because it isn't fighting but rather conflict *avoidance* and the ensuing disconnection that threatens most romantic partnerships.

Simply put: Staying quiet in the face of conflict destroys relationships.

We Are Terrified of Conflict

It's normal to fear conflict. And not just fear it—*avoid* it, at all costs. Conflict is uncomfortable, it can be scary, and it seems guaranteed to cause harm. We've been taught that conflict is a sign that our relationships aren't working. If we're in conflict, doesn't that mean our relationship is broken?

Actually it's the opposite. Conflict, as we'll discover in these pages, is healthy (even inevitable) when two people come together with different backgrounds, personalities, wants, and needs. But not all conflict is created equal. There is a difference between destructive conflict (which is unproductive and damaging) and healthy conflict (in which partners communicate consciously and honestly). Healthy conflict offers an opportunity for growth and intimacy. If you can navigate it effectively, you can harness its potential—to feel closer to your partner than you ever imagined and develop your own emotional maturity in the process.

Healthy conflict *saves* marriages; it doesn't destroy them.

But that's a tough message for many women to believe. They've spent their whole lives avoiding conflict and sidestepping difficult emotions, especially in their romantic relationships. I hear hundreds of women from all walks of life saying the same thing as my client Anna did: *I should have spoken up sooner.*

What's surprising to many of these women is that before starting couples therapy and facing these communication issues head on, many of them would have *thought* of themselves as emotionally astute and communicative. They are the moms who are there for their kids to lean on when they've had a bad day at school. They are the friends who are supportive when a pal is going through a rough patch. They are the daughters who show up when they're needed. But when it comes to their closest romantic relationships, they wake up and realize they've been avoiding the hard stuff for too long—months, years, maybe even longer. And now they're not sure if things can be repaired.

Some women have been extremely vocal in their relationship, but not in the ways that truly allow them to be heard. Criticizing, nitpicking, and blaming are all forms of ineffective communication and avoidance of the underlying issues. Other women have stuffed down their feelings and silenced themselves, convinced their true thoughts and opinions aren't valid—whether it's those small, daily disappointments in their relationship that are easy to sweep under the rug, or bigger issues that feel too overwhelming to navigate. Believe it or not, *both* are forms of conflict avoidance . . . and once the women I've worked with learn about this epidemic, they realize they too had essentially "quiet-quit" their relationship years before, when they stopped communicating about their deeper feelings and needs. Not only had they compromised their relationships, but worse, they had sacrificed their own sense of well-being in the process.

That is the true cost of being quiet: You abandon your essential self to keep the peace. It is the profound loss that comes from trading long-term intimacy, growth, and personal happiness for the short-term comfort of avoiding what needs to be said. Ultimately, you're missing out on emotional intimacy, truly knowing your partner and yourself, and inviting your partner to know you more deeply.

The tricky thing is that you may not even realize this emotional gulf is widening, or how you're contributing to it, until it's too late. Until one day, a crisis occurs that impacts your relationship: a physical or emotional affair, a hardship with your child, an illness or a struggle with addiction. It could even be one infinitesimally small last straw that finally exposes the gulf of disconnection and can no longer be ignored. You wake up one day and discover that you don't know your partner anymore, and there's really nothing left between you but memories and a shared address.

Do any of these scenarios sound familiar to you?

- Do you crave more connection and emotional intimacy but don't know how to get it?
- Do you struggle with how to effectively communicate what you feel and need?
- Do you avoid bringing up difficult topics because it never seems to go well?
- Does it ever feel like you have only two crappy choices—to avoid conflict or get in a fight?
- Do you ever feel like you're not really seen or heard in your relationship? Do you allow this feeling to shut you down and prevent you from speaking up?
- Do you immerse yourself in work, children, socializing, or some other distraction to avoid that feeling of disconnection from your partner?

- Have you convinced yourself that you *would* bring up the hard things if only your partner would listen and respond differently?
- Maybe you don't want your relationship to end and could never imagine blowing up your whole life . . . but living in an emotionally disconnected relationship feels deeply unsatisfying, too.

If you relate to any of this, whether a little or a lot, there is something you can do about it. There are healthy ways to speak up for your needs that can prevent long-term damage to your relationship. The important thing is to address it *now*. If you wait for a true crisis point—a day when things are so profoundly disconnected between you and your partner that you can't see a way back together—it might be too late to finally speak up. Your relationship may end, even if that's the last thing you ever wanted.

It doesn't have to be that way, though.

Relationships are our greatest resource. Research shows that having close, secure bonds doesn't just enhance the quality of our lives but actually determines how long we live. That's worth fighting for. And you might be amazed at what's possible when you stop avoiding your partner and start showing up again in your relationship. That's the only thing you can control: your own behavior. But when you change what you do, your connection with your partner can dramatically improve.

I've seen countless relationships transform when one partner stops avoiding conflict and starts meaningfully engaging in the relationship. I've watched long-entrenched dynamics change when one person uses the skills I've taught them to finally speak up. Intimacy, joy, freedom, confidence, secure attachment, and rediscovery—that's what happens when people learn to be vulnerable, honest, and open—when they know how to identify what they feel and share it.

Of course, I can't guarantee that your partner will meet all your needs or fulfill you. But I do know that if you're not speaking up on your own behalf, you'll never know what's possible. Regardless of what you discover, you'll be emotionally liberated by transmitting your true feelings. And there's power—even beauty, and great bravery as well—in inviting your partner to know who you really are at the core. If, after that process, you discover that your relationship still can't be what you want . . . well, then you'll have the information you need to make informed choices about your future. Either way, you'll know you've done all that you can do.

And most important, you won't abandon yourself and your own needs to keep the peace. Because that's the greatest cost—denying yourself the chance to express what you really feel. Here's what I want you to know before we move forward into unlocking your authentic voice:

- Your needs matter.
- You deserve to speak up for them.
- Communicating like a mature adult is challenging but worth it.
- You can do it.

I'm going to show you how.

What You'll Get Out of This Book

Through years of working with couples on these very issues of conflict avoidance and connection, I've developed a tried-and-true method I call Self-Connected Communication—it's the antidote to the conflict avoidance and disconnection I see in so many of my clients. With Self-

Connected Communication, I help couples go beyond the surface-level issues to find their voices, share their deeper feelings and needs, and create true emotional intimacy.

Before you can learn to overcome conflict avoidance, though, you'll need to dig into the *why* of it all. In Part I, you'll learn how you might be avoiding things that need to be said and why it's so easy to get stuck in dead-end arguments.

Then, in Part II, we'll dive into the first phase of Self-Connected Communication—unlocking your authentic voice. I'll teach you what healthy communication actually looks like, how to know you've been triggered, and how to pause and process your internal experience so you have the clarity you need to communicate effectively. Essentially, this first phase of Self-Connected Communication is all about doing the *inner* work so you can show up as your best, most authentic self once you start communicating to your partner.

Finally, in Part III, we'll move into the second phase of Self-Connected Communication—using the voice you just found to speak up in your relationship. In these final chapters you'll learn how to start approaching your partner with a clear constructive message—one that can lead to connection and growth. We'll cover how to empower yourself to use your voice consistently, what it looks like when you speak up in your everyday life, what to do when you don't get the response you were hoping for from your partner, and how to make this a habit. By the end of this book, you'll be armed with all the tools you need to foster the relationships you desire and, more important, deserve.

If this seems daunting, I understand. Because I've been there, too.

This book is informed by what I've learned from trial and error in my own personal life. What many of my clients don't know is that I once lost my own voice, many years ago in my first marriage. I saw myself as an excellent communicator but could not for the life of me figure out how to speak up clearly and effectively about my needs. And by the time my husband and I got into therapy, we were so disconnected that it was too late. We divorced after seven years of marriage.

That painful experience inspired me to become a couples therapist. I had a mission to help people learn to show up differently for their relationships and themselves—so they didn't get to that place of disempowerment and despair that I did. In doing so, I discovered that feeling bitter, defeated, and resentful is entirely preventable. Although I don't know what would have happened with my first marriage if I had spoken up sooner, I do know I would have felt so much healthier, happier, and self-assured if I'd known how to use my voice. Ultimately, I wrote this book to offer you the information I wish I'd had back then. As we move through this vulnerable journey together, I promise to be transparent with you about my own past struggles and my continued efforts to practice what I preach in my current marriage.

Communicating with a primary romantic partner is a constant work in progress. We are wired to seek connection with our spouse (so we have the urge to talk about everything, even the hard things), but we also fear the *loss* of that connection (so we shy away from sharing the difficult topics, afraid that we'll be *too much* or this problem will be *too scary* for our relationship to weather). Yet with effort, we can improve and evolve. We can learn to override our natural impulses to avoid what's uncomfortable and take the risk to communicate in the vulnerable ways that bring us closer to the person we love.

Here's what you can expect to learn in *The Cost of Quiet*:

- Understand how and why avoidant behaviors take hold
- Understand what's really happening in conflict with your partner

- Develop a healthy relationship mindset and take responsibility for your behavior
- Become more aware of unconscious dynamics and unhealed hurts
- Tune in to deeper feelings as a guide to your needs
- Understand your attachment fears and how to manage them
- Understand protective strategies and what to do differently
- Know how to pause and process before initiating communication
- Approach your partner in ways that give you the best chance of being heard
- Distill what you need to share with your partner
- Express yourself with vulnerability, assertiveness, honesty, and kindness
- Self-soothe, initiate repair, and create boundaries
- Make a habit of using your voice effectively

How to Use This Book

Each chapter will have real-world case examples that are composites of the many clients I've worked with over the years, and questions for reflection. There are also exercises throughout the book that will deepen your learnings. You might want to start a journal devoted to Self-Connected Communication, so you can capture your insights and review them.

However, these are skills that rely on commitment and daily practice, not just insight. Your gains will depend on the degree to which you dig in and interact with the material—doing the exercises, making notes, and trying new behaviors. It's a lifelong journey to work with powerful emotions, connect with another person through them, and show up like a mature adult. It's not always easy, but it's worth it. And it's a journey you can successfully embark on as soon as you start reading the first chapter.

Please note that although this book has been written for women in committed relationships, the methods herein are applicable to all and meant to be inclusive. I've used the pronoun *they* for the sake of simplicity and to make sure everyone can find themself in the text.

You can create a relationship of depth, meaning, and fulfillment. It all starts with facing—not avoiding—the challenging conversations and difficult work of connecting to yourself and your partner. So let's get started and let the changes begin!

PART I

Why We Lose Our Voice and Avoid Conflict

CHAPTER 1

What Self-Silencing and Avoidant Behavior Look Like

Morgan and Leo sit on my couch, as far apart as possible. Morgan is perched on the edge of her seat, staring out the window. I note a faint tremble in her chin. The tissue box, one of two that I have stationed on either side of the couch in my office, sits perched on her lap, ready for the tears she's obviously holding back as she struggles to still her hands. Leo sits with his arms crossed and his jaw clenched, his knee bouncing like a jackhammer. I can feel the tension radiating off him as if he were just cooked in a microwave.

Morgan had called to schedule an initial session with me two days after Leo discovered she'd been having an affair. Now she looks like she's about to throw up, and he looks like he's about to start screaming. I wouldn't expect it any other way.

Emotions are always running high in these situations, and I know I'll need to work hard to create safety in the room. As I begin gently connecting with each of them and exploring their individual perspectives, a painful but all-too-common story begins to emerge.

Leo recounts what happened, the words tumbling out. An incriminating text had come in while he was using Morgan's phone, and he'd immediately called that number, then heard a guy answer and quickly hang up. He'd confronted Morgan, who had initially lied but eventually confessed to an astonishing betrayal that had blown his mind.

Morgan admitted she'd reconnected with a high school boyfriend who'd recently gotten a divorce. It had started out innocently enough—two old friends catching up on the past twenty years and reminiscing about old times—but had gradually slipped over the line into the kind of intimate sharing that constitutes an emotional affair. Eventually, the daily phone calls and texting banter led to sharing explicit photos and an in-person encounter. It then spiraled into a full-blown physical affair—one that had been ongoing for nearly one year.

At first glance it might seem as if their marital problems are all about Morgan's infidelity—and certainly the fallout from that will have to be dealt with. But in fact the real culprit here is the profound disconnection that happened between them *long* before any cheating took place. Over the next few sessions, I learn more about their respective histories, what first drew them to each other, and what brought them to this moment.

Morgan and Leo are in their late thirties and have two children—Max, age eleven, and Abigail, age eight. They have been married for twelve years. Morgan always loved that Leo was tall, handsome, and confident; when they met (at a university dive bar their junior year of college), Leo had come right up to her, introduced himself, and offered to buy her a drink. For his part, Leo remembered being immediately drawn to the bright, bubbly Morgan, and he'd quickly discovered that she was as kind and mild-mannered as she was pretty. They'd felt a spark between them, instant and intense.

More important, as they got to know each other, they discovered they had the exact same goals, values, and vision for their lives. They both wanted to have a traditional home life, where Morgan would stay home with the kids while they were young. So that's exactly what she did—a few years after graduation, after she gave birth to Max, she'd quit her job in PR and become a stay-at-home mother. They felt fortunate that Leo's job as an engineer afforded them this luxury, and for a while things went smoothly. They took nice vacations every year; their kids were healthy and doing well in school. From the outside looking in, they seemed to have it all. So what had gone wrong?

....

They'd been in agreement about this recipe for a perfect life, and it had all seemed to be working out just as they'd planned. But somewhere along the way, that shared vision changed. Morgan had been feeling stifled by stay-at-home life and longed for adult interaction and stimulation—not to mention the sense of accomplishment she'd gotten from her career. She was often overwhelmed by taking care of the kids and having little to no hands-on help from Leo, who seemed too preoccupied with work to connect with her emotionally. After years of this, Morgan felt lonely, confused, and resentful. Then, she had cheated . . . leading this "perfect" couple to my office, on the brink of divorce.

After counseling countless couples through this exact issue, I can predict with a fair degree of certainty that Morgan has been unconsciously avoiding the hard conversations for a long, long time. Now that that avoidant behavior has brought them here, it's time to get to the bottom of it to properly move forward.

The True Cost of Avoidant Behavior

The idea that cheating automatically indicates that something is flawed or lacking in a relationship is a myth long perpetuated by society, both out of sheer ignorance and because it feels safer for people to believe they have some control over circumstances and can prevent such a painful thing from happening to them. In other words, we'd like to believe that if you're a good partner and give all you have to your relationship, you won't get cheated on.

Try telling that to Leo.

The truth is, cheating happens for all kinds of reasons:

- We're human and naturally attracted to others throughout our lifespan.
- We can get close to other people without realizing that we're drifting into dangerous territory.
- We get lonely, bored, insecure, and desperate for attention and validation.
- We've avoided the real, underlying problems in our primary relationship for too long.

Despite these nuances, there is one central truth: If you and your partner are emotionally connected and there's honest, open communication, cheating is much, *much* less likely to happen. If conversely, like in Morgan's case, you avoid talking about your needs and feelings for fear of what might come out of those discussions—disconnection, or potential infidelity, will be the result.

In most cases, though, conflict avoidance isn't something you wake up and actively choose to do. No one wants to hide or miscommunicate their feelings with their partner! It stems from many unconscious micro decisions that ultimately lead to harmful disconnection in your relationship.

Avoidant behaviors range from suppressing feelings and self-silencing to loudly projecting blame and anger. It might look like telling your partner you're fine when you're actually seething because you're convinced they can't handle hearing what you have to say—or maybe you don't trust yourself to say it without getting ugly. It may look like allowing frustration to boil over into an explosion of damaging insults you don't really mean and can't take back. It can also take the form of incessant bickering or passive-aggressive digs. All of these avoidant behaviors (which we'll break down later in this chapter) obfuscate the underlying feelings and needs that you *must* share in order to have a healthy connected relationship.

We can slip into this avoidant behavior the minute there's tension in the air. Let's face it, it can be uncomfortable to have those hard conversations with your partner when you're not sure how they will receive and respond to them. However, when you choose avoidant behavior, you sabotage your relationship and get stuck in what I call **the avoidance trap**. Essentially, you prioritize the short-term comfort of avoidance over the long-term benefits of intimacy and growth that stem from constructively addressing conflict. Avoidant behaviors feel good in the moment because they prevent the anxiety that naturally occurs when you take the risk to be vulnerable—but the more you avoid, the more deeply ensnared you are in the trap, making it even harder to speak up and create meaningful connection with your partner.

Simply put: Avoidant behavior is what kills relationships. Not the issues or underlying feelings themselves, but choosing not to face them. Like Morgan and Leo, you can be stuck in that trap for a long time without knowing what's happening until a crisis hits or it's too late.

Good communication doesn't automatically make you or your partner impervious to attraction to other people. It doesn't mean that it's impossible for an outside force to threaten your relationship. But it does mean you will be *less* vulnerable to letting an attraction get out of hand if you learn how to speak up about your needs and communicate with each other—and yes, even fight!—clearly and often. If you have a relationship in which you and your partner know how to address conflict, then you'll be able to talk about it if either one of you starts to feel disconnected, lonely, or attracted to someone else . . . as difficult as it might be to hear that.

Staying quiet and avoiding problems in your relationship doesn't mean they go away. Quite the opposite.

Avoidance Breeds Resentment

As Morgan opens up to me in our one-on-one session, it becomes clear that she had silenced herself and avoided her true feelings in this relationship for a long, long time. She is steeped in remorse, regret, and shame about her actions, but as we dig deeper together, she confirms my early hypothesis: that the seeds of this affair had begun with her own self-silencing, people-pleasing tendencies, and avoidant behaviors, *years* before there was any contact with her old boyfriend.

"How did you and Leo handle conflict before the affair?" I ask in an early session.

"Honestly, we didn't," she tells me. "We avoided it completely. Early on I tried to bring up certain feelings, but it never seemed to go well and I probably wasn't clear. It's really hard for me to ask for what I need."

Morgan explains that this lack of communication intensified after their children were born—when she felt that the mental and physical load of parenting and all the household responsibilities fell on her. Her frustration over the unfair disparity between their domestic duties grew. When she did try to communicate, however minimally and indirectly, she felt Leo was dismissive or defensive, pointing to all the things he did to help support her. Then she'd tell herself that maybe she was just being selfish and she should be putting her kids and partner first.

"He wasn't understanding me, or would tell me all the reasons I *shouldn't* feel that way. Then I'd feel even more upset and confused and question if I was even justified in feeling how I felt," she says.

She didn't want to fight—and nothing seemed to change, anyway—so she just gave up.

"I had all this resentment, and it just grew and grew. It didn't seem like there was anything I could do about it," she explains, tears rolling down her face that she doesn't bother wiping away.

Morgan had fallen into what I call **the cave of resentment**—a familiar effect of the avoidance trap that I often see with my clients. It goes like this: When you avoid conflict, it's as if you're walking through a sunny meadow toward a beautiful, cozy cottage. Then you unexpectedly fall through a hole in the ground you didn't see and land in a cold, dark cave.

At first you try hard to get out, but every pathway you attempt is either obscured or seems too dangerous to traverse, so eventually you just sit down and give up, resigned to being stuck alone in that cave unless someone comes along to rescue you.

Meanwhile, there is a solution available to you that you've failed to notice. You've been darting back and forth, frantically trying to find a way out, but had never thought to look back up at the hole you fell in through. If you were exploring with curiosity, you would surely see that there is a little ladder right there along the wall leading up and into the light.

At first glance the ladder looks too steep, as if it's too rickety to climb. It doesn't feel safe, but the alternative is to stay in this lonely, dark, miserable place forever, so you decide to give it a shot. The first step is filled with terror, and you expect to fall, but you keep going.

Slowly but surely you make your way up, gaining confidence one rung at a time.

This is what happens when you learn to speak up in your relationship. You tap into your own internal wellspring of power and confidence to effectively communicate your feelings and needs. As a result, you stay out of, or save yourself from, the avoidance trap.

Prior to the affair, Morgan had fallen victim to the avoidance trap and was stuck in that cave of resentment, not knowing she had a way out.

When I meet with Leo for his one-on-one session, we briefly touch on his perspective of this pre-affair time. Understandably, it's tough for him to push past the pain of the affair to reflect on the past. His emotions vacillate from shock to anger, between a desire to divorce her immediately and an urge to beg her to choose him and stay. There is also a compulsion to blame himself for her affair and question what *he* did wrong, a sentiment that I often hear in these early days after a disclosure. Of course, all of these big feelings and questions must be dealt with. But perhaps the important piece of this puzzle to address, if this couple wants to heal and move forward together, is how a lack of communication over the long term contributed to the enormous rupture they now face.

I ask Leo what Morgan had communicated to him about her feelings prior to the affair. I am wondering if he'd had any sense of how frustrated and resentful she had been feeling.

"She seemed a little overwhelmed sometimes around stuff with the kids, but that's just normal at this stage of life, right? I didn't think any of it was that big of a deal. I thought she was happy with our life," he says. "I can't even think of a time we really argued. I didn't even *know* she was upset about anything!"

Leo's brain goes over this fundamental disconnect again and again. Morgan is saying things were bad for her for a long time. But he can't reconcile that with what *he* saw, both before and throughout her year-long affair: a woman who seemed content and hadn't said a word about deep fissures, dissatisfactions, or unmet emotional needs. Morgan was right: She hadn't been clear about what she was feeling and needing, and her indirect attempts hadn't registered with Leo at all.

Morgan has to take responsibility for having an affair, and she will have to work hard for a long time to repair that injury with Leo if that's indeed what she wants. Infidelity, whether physical or emotional, is known as **an attachment injury**: a deep, emotional wound to a couple's bond that damages trust and creates insecurity. It takes lots of time, patience, and hard work to make the bond secure again. But often infidelity is preceded by periods of *emotional* estrangement such as this. Morgan had long felt that Leo was too busy to be there for her, so she had talked herself into avoiding conflict and suppressing her deeper feelings and needs to keep the peace. And indeed, Leo hadn't recognized what were in retrospect signs that his wife was struggling, such as being less affectionate and more withdrawn. The distance and disconnection in their relationship that existed prior to the affair—indeed, that *contributed* to the affair—is something Morgan and Leo co-created, because they had avoided communicating about the hard things.

The Curse of the "Good Girl"

I see so many women like Morgan, who have worn the identity of good wife and mother so thoroughly that they've stopped speaking up for the needs of their authentic selves. Each of us has a wise, loving, adult part of ourselves, an inner voice that knows what we need. If only we listen, that voice can guide us with an intuitive, internal compass. Morgan, however, had barely ever acknowledged her true emotional needs and didn't yet understand how she got herself to this point. She'd carried the bulk of the logistical and emotional labor for her family for years, as so many women do, and had tried to say something early on, in muted, indirect ways. But when she couldn't get through to Leo, she had given up and "gone quiet." What followed were years of self-sacrificing and stuffing her own feelings and needs down in order to keep the peace. She'd become a pro at making her husband and kids happy . . . often at her own expense.

She'd long suffered from a classic case of good-girl-itis: a highly contagious people-pleasing disease that often comes from what's modeled in our families of origin and conditioned by a society that still punishes women for "being difficult" when we speak up and create waves. We absorb all of this nonsense by osmosis, without realizing we're breathing in some seriously poisoned gas. The most insidious part: We lie to ourselves that we have to keep the peace and sacrifice for others, instead of owning that it's a costly choice we're imposing on ourselves.

I'm in recovery from a bad case of good-girl-itis myself. I like to joke that I finally, after a lot of hard work, graduated from Anti-People-Pleasing University (APPU), where "good girls" go to be deconditioned. I picture this place like a campus from an old episode of *The Twilight Zone*, where women stagger in zombielike, with spinning red pinwheels in their eyes, chanting the phrase "My needs don't matter; I live to make others happy." After lots of study, group discussion, and reading, and a ton of self-reflection, though, graduates of APPU can come out confident, just like I did. We find ourselves saying assertive, clear, self-focused things about our own needs, like "I care about you, but my needs matter, too," and, just simply and powerfully, "No." We walk out reprogrammed for the better, with eyes now clear and full of vibrancy, as we are in touch with and connected to ourselves.

Today, fully cured of good-girl-itis and with my Anti-People-Pleasing diploma firmly in hand, I know how to share my deeper feelings and core needs. I know that expressing them keeps me healthy inside. I know that it's my responsibility to care for my own vulnerable inner child this way, too . . . but I didn't always know this. I used to have a nearly terminal case of good-girl-itis, and what Morgan doesn't know as she cries on the couch in my office is how much I can relate to her story on a personal level. She might be shocked to learn how thoroughly I'd contributed to the demise of my own first marriage by silencing myself.

....

Let me take you back to a moment more than twenty years ago.

I clutched the baby monitor, listening for the faintest sound that I'd have to run to the nursery. Two wet coins of breast milk formed on my unwashed T-shirt. Tears ran down my face and dripped off my chin. My husband sat on the couch, his tie loosened after a long workday, with the remote control in one hand and a glass of wine in the other as he chuckled at a commercial on the Golf Channel. He was right there beside me, but he was miles away.

I'd been a wreck since my first daughter was born and, in some ways, even before that, as I'd had a miscarriage shortly before I got pregnant with her. I was very young, living far away from my family, and recovering from a traumatic labor that had endangered both of our lives and left my daughter unable to breathe when she was first born. My body felt like a split cantaloupe that had been dropped on the ground and left to ooze and rot.

In that moment on the couch, a hamster wheel of worries cranked through my mind on overdrive—the baby could suffocate on the bumper; she might not get enough breast milk; what if she got too much milk and choked from reflux? On and on and on it went. She barely slept at night, so I barely slept at all. I hadn't known it was possible to love someone so much and feel so overwhelmed by trying to care for her properly.

I needed help.

I got up from the couch and stepped into my husband's line of sight, blocking him from seeing a Tiger Woods victory moment onscreen. "I'm drowning here," I pleaded.

"What?" he said. "Just sleep when she sleeps during the day; you don't have to go to work anymore." Then he reached around me with the remote to adjust the volume. "And besides, I even got you a night nurse, so there should be no problem. She's fine. You're fine. Just relax."

But I wasn't fine. The message I got from my husband was that he'd given me everything I could possibly need and that it was supremely irritating that I couldn't seem to appreciate it, much less just be okay.

In a sense he was right. He had given me everything—everything except the most essential, fundamental thing I really longed for: *him*.

How could I explain that I needed him to crawl into the trenches with me and hold my hand through the rugged, unfamiliar terrain? I didn't know how to ask for that, or that it was *okay* to ask for that.

I began to doubt my own needs. Now the cracks in what had seemed like a perfect relationship began to show. As I looked at my partner there on the couch that night, our first daughter only a few weeks old, the anger fueled by loneliness began heating up inside me like a coil on the stove.

Oddly enough, when I met my husband in college, it was this very lack of emotionalism that had appealed to me. My parents had fought constantly for years before they finally divorced. To find solace, I had escaped to the peaceful homes of my Catholic school friends—none of whom would have even considered divorce an option—where everything was ultra-genteel and "please-pass-the-butter-ish" and so, so unlike the chaos and vitriol that festered in my own home. I learned that conflict is *bad* and should be avoided. I vowed that I would grow up to have the happiest marriage ever with no fighting, just like my friends' parents, many of whom, I realized years later, were probably miserable and just didn't show it. For me that meant not being "needy" but instead "going with the flow," with a smile on my face—which is not my true personality at all.

Over the years, I found that when I did approach my husband, his responses were distant and dismissive. It felt like my only choice was to stop saying the things that he didn't seem to want to hear. But this avoidance led only to an empty, lonely feeling that grew in my gut and intensified with time.

As I got older and started to really know myself, I discovered that I wanted connection more than I wanted to avoid conflict. I began to realize that what I'd thought would be perfect was really just a surface relationship—a relationship that makes for a great Christmas card with lots of external fun but lacks the depth and substance that makes a relationship feel real and grounded. I wanted my relationship to have depth and meaning; I wanted to be able to open up, share myself, and feel known, valued, and accepted. I wanted to be able to express my needs and not feel like I was defective for having them, but I didn't know how to do that.

Avoidance as a Coping Strategy

When I talk about women "going quiet," I am specifically referring to being quiet about your true, vulnerable feelings and needs in your relationship, just as I did in my first marriage. "Quiet" is a euphemism for conflict avoidance. It's avoiding talking about the hard stuff that must be addressed for both your own well-being and the good of your relationship.

Women specifically self-silence as a coping strategy to keep the peace and avoid self-expression that could lead to conflict. We'll delve into the why of it all much more in the next chapter, but I want you to understand very clearly that you cannot and will not feel good inside over the long run if you're not communicating your deeper feelings and needs in your relationship.

You'll also have zero chance of having a healthy, secure, emotionally connected relationship. The best you'll get is a relationship like mine was—one that looks decent from the outside and floats along at the surface without much depth or substance. That would be like living on a diet of nothing but soda and peanut butter cups for years. You might survive, and it might taste good going down, but you're going to feel sick and malnourished and probably suffer organ failure over time. I had to learn the hard way—by making tons of mistakes, going through a divorce, unpacking my role in the collapse of my marriage in therapy, and spending years training to be a counselor. Now that I'm a couples therapist, I want to share the tools and perspective I wish I'd had at the time, so others don't have to struggle the way I did.

As a couples therapist, I've come to see that avoiding conflict, while all too human and understandable, ironically *becomes* the biggest source of conflict over the long term. When you don't speak up about your feelings and needs in an effort to avoid conflict, you create the very distance and disconnection you wish to avoid. Avoiding the problem *becomes* the problem. When you stay quiet, you're sacrificing your own self-care, self-advocacy, and personal growth to keep the peace, and you wind up feeling lonely, disempowered, and stuck in that cave of resentment, not realizing that you can, and must, climb out.

Quiet doesn't necessarily always sound so quiet, either. I never would have self-identified as quiet—rather, I'm an extreme extrovert who talks constantly (unless I'm in session or sleeping)! I will get into meaty conversations with everyone, from the grocery store clerk to the person next to me in line at the DMV, if given the chance. Beyond this, I'm extremely adept at being assertive in other areas of my life; no one has ever accused me of being a shrinking violet. Like me, many women don't necessarily see themselves as quiet or realize they're avoiding conflict. Let's delve into more of what avoidant behavior can look and sound like as a coping strategy in relationships.

The Top Ten Avoidant Coping Strategies

Some or all, of these avoidant coping strategies can be used instead of speaking up and engaging in conflict directly with your partner.

1. **Outsourcing needs for connection:** It's normal to crave emotional intimacy; in fact it's a fundamental relationship need. If it's lacking, you may overinvest in other relationships in an attempt to fill the void. Some women spend most of their time with their kids or their friends, sharing their innermost thoughts in those relationships instead of with their partners. Others, like Morgan, turn to emotional or physical affairs for the connection they're missing.

2. **Distracting and/or numbing:** There are lots of ways you may distract yourself from what's bothering you in your relationship. You might throw yourself into working too much, compulsive shopping, hobbies, social media, and other addictive tendencies, such as drinking alcohol or smoking pot, in an attempt to self-soothe. These avoidant behaviors prevent you from confronting the issues at hand.

3. **People-pleasing and appeasing ("good-girl-itis"):** In relationships, people-pleasing can take various forms and all of them are avoidant. You may say yes to things you don't want to do, fail to establish boundaries, try to manage your partner's emotions, and neglect yourself by focusing on your partner. These all have something in common—sacrificing your wants and needs to keep the peace and letting true self-care fall by the wayside.

4. **Criticizing and blaming:** You may try to communicate about what's bothering you but tend to express it with criticism and blame. This is one of the most common ways women avoid speaking up about their true feelings and core needs. It's finger-pointing and focusing on what you *don't* like about your partner instead of sharing about yourself. This is often delivered in a constant, dripping-faucet style, such as nagging or nitpicking.

5. **Hyper-independence:** Many women pride themselves on their hyper-independence, not realizing it's a form of avoidance. Underneath that pride lurks the belief that you can't count on your partner anyway, so why bother asking for help? "Never mind, I'll handle it myself" is the mentality, as you deny your own needs and thereby eliminate the possibility of having them met.

6. **Compartmentalizing or shutting down:** Another way to avoid conflict is to disconnect by putting your emotions in a box and sealing it tight. This allows you to ignore the problem completely—out of sight, out of mind. You may wall yourself off from your feelings or shut down emotionally from your partner because you expect to be disappointed and just don't want to go there.

7. **"Victim volcano" syndrome:** Sometimes instead of compartmentalizing, women stuff feelings until they implode. Perceiving yourself as a victim of your partner's actions, you're angry but avoid discussing your grievances. The tension builds inside you until you can't take it anymore. Then *boom!* The resulting explosion is often disproportionate to the level of wrongdoing, leaving your partner shocked and confused by your reaction.

8. **Passive-aggressiveness:** Passive-aggressiveness is covert communication that masks how upset you are. You avoid expressing your true feelings and instead make snide jokes or throw barbs, pretending they're innocent comments. By disguising them, you don't own your feelings or reveal them directly, so although your partner can tell you're upset, they don't know why, or what you really mean, feel, or need.

9. **Bickering:** Bickering is an avoidant coping strategy because it never allows you and your partner to delve into true and deep self-disclosure. When you engage in light back-and-forth arguing about petty frustrations, you never get beyond the surface level. With this approach, your issues are never resolved in a satisfactory way.

10. **Sweeping frustrations under the rug:** Perhaps the most common and pervasive type of avoidance is sweeping conflict under the rug. You may ignore problems and brush them away before they even register. Instead of talking about them or even compartmentalizing, you wait for the tension to blow over and simply move on. There can be no understanding or repair because

the existence of an issue has never been acknowledged in the first place.

These avoidant strategies typically coexist and overlap, meaning you may use one or all of them in different scenarios. I've been known to deploy every single one of these tactics, but criticizing and victim volcano syndrome are probably the greatest hits on my own personal avoidance soundtrack (spoiler: We all have one!). I never *intend* to be critical of my husband, but that's not how it comes out on the surface. When something I say comes out critically—meaning when it focuses on the other person rather than on me and my experience—I am much less likely to get the response I want, much less get my needs met. It's a lesson I, and many others, have to learn over and over again.

Each of these avoidant coping strategies is destructive, and they have these three things in common:

1. You're dealing only with surface feelings or not dealing with feelings at all.
2. You're not expressing your core needs and may not even be aware of them.
3. You're using an inner dialogue based on distorted thoughts or false beliefs, lying to yourself that you have no choice but to avoid conflict in this way.

All of these strategies conspire to keep you from revealing what needs to be said.

Yet one way or another, your feelings and needs will fight to be heard. They'll keep knocking at the door of your consciousness until you listen and start climbing out of the cave. Now that you're aware of this, you might catch yourself saying one or more of these common phrases to justify your silence and remain in the cave:

- It's no big deal.
- It won't matter even if I say something.
- They don't care, so why bother?
- They won't get it anyway.
- It's silly.
- It's stupid.
- I'm being selfish.
- I'm being too critical.
- It's not worth a fight.
- I shouldn't feel this way.
- I can't say it because it will upset my partner.

Do any of these statements sound familiar to you? Is there a part of you that whispers these self-deceptions to yourself in key moments of potential conflict, perhaps so quietly you're not even aware?

If so, you're deluding yourself into avoiding conflict and self-silencing to keep the peace. The part of you that says these things or something like them is a protective part that is trying to keep you from getting hurt, as we'll explore in upcoming chapters.

The Antidote to Avoidance

Everyone has the capacity to communicate their feelings and needs effectively. But it can be scary at first because it's new, and it feels like exercising an unused muscle. As you practice, you will build your own emotional muscle and get better and better at effective *interpersonal* communication. You'll discover that the lived reality of these moments is far less scary than the anticipation of these moments. Yes, read that again. *The anticipation of the fearful thing is harder than the thing itself.*

Being vulnerable about your feelings and needs is scary, and if you show up and communicate in this openhearted way, you may indeed get hurt or disappointed. But you will also realize that you can handle it. You'll come to understand that it feels better inside you when you speak up for yourself, even if your partner can't or won't respond well. You're going to learn how to communicate effectively about your feelings and needs so that you feel better—both inside you and inside your relationship, even when your partner doesn't agree with you, doesn't respond to your requests as you'd like, or doesn't really hear you or get it. (This last option is not the ideal, but in real life that's sometimes what happens.)

The only way to get this discovery into your bones is to try it yourself and experience how it feels. When you're practicing Self-Connected Communication in Part II, your nervous system will begin to understand that it's not as scary as you thought it would be. It gets easier and easier, one small interaction at a time.

There is no magical solution or perfect way of saying things that guarantee you get heard, but when you take care of yourself by using your voice and speaking your truth, you avoid falling into the cave of resentment. As a result, you feel more confident, empowered, and clear. You have information about what your relationship can and cannot offer you and you can make the choices that best serve you. You take care of your inner child like the wise, loving adult you are, and you know what? *It feels good.* This is something you must do for you, and actually, as you'll come to see, it's simpler than you might think.

HOW DO YOU AVOID CONFLICT?

Close your eyes, take a couple of cleansing breaths, and let yourself settle in and get grounded. Now bring your mind's eye to a recent occasion when you were frustrated or upset with your partner.

Watch the scene as if it were a movie.

What do you see yourself doing and hear yourself saying in relation to your partner?

Do you notice yourself engaged in any of the top ten avoidant coping strategies from this chapter?

What were you saying to yourself on the inside that you're not saying outside?

What is your inner voice telling you about what's happening with your partner at that moment?

There is no right or wrong answer. Just see what you notice as this scene plays out, and keep those avoidant coping strategies in mind as you keep reading.

Please note that if you've been through significant childhood trauma, this will likely be harder for you, and you'll need to move more slowly and take smaller risks with your partner as you build muscle for vulnerable communication. As always, if anything we discuss in these pages ever feels too uncomfortable for you to handle on your own, honor your intuition and don't proceed without consulting a therapist.

Questions for Reflection

- As you pictured yourself handling this recent conflict, what did you notice about how you expressed your feelings and needs?

- Did you stuff your feelings or push them down inside?
- Did you feel reluctant to engage in conflict with your partner?
- Did you avoid expressing yourself in some way?
- What did you learn in this exercise about how you handle conflict with your partner?

CHAPTER 2

What's Really Going On in Relationships When We Avoid Conflict

"I'm not even sure we need to be here," my client Grace said when she first walked into my office nearly a year ago with a polite smile and a reluctant spouse trailing in her wake.

"Yeah, we don't really have any issues, and I don't see the point of doing counseling," her husband, Andrew, was quick to add.

I waited, giving them space to share more.

"I mean she doesn't really seem to like me, but I'm sure that's the way it goes for lots of husbands, right?" Andrew threw up his hands in a what-can-you-do kind of shrug and chuckled.

Oof. I could see that the laughter covered real pain. Clearly they did have issues, and there was nothing funny about them.

Grace, a forty-eight-year-old woman from Boston, had started dating Andrew, a fifty-year-old from Queens, New York, in medical school in the 1990s. They had relocated to Orlando, Florida, after they completed their medical residencies. Andrew worked for a large hospital as a pulmonologist, and Grace ran a thriving dermatology practice with five offices throughout the metro area. They had been married for sixteen years and had three boys: Benji, fourteen; Luke, twelve; and Kai, ten. Both parents worked demanding jobs but were also devoted to their kids, who did well in school, played various sports, and seemed reasonably well-adjusted.

Grace explained, "Look, we get crabby with each other and have petty little squabbles sometimes, but mostly everything is fine. We share the same values, we agree on the big issues, and we have a great life."

I leaned in, sensing she was about to reveal the source of her own pain, the core reason for coming to couples therapy.

"Despite all that, I just don't feel connected," she sighed, shaking her head while picking a thread off her immaculate cream slacks.

As I began to probe their dynamic in that first session, I could see that this couple didn't realize what was driving their disconnection.

Women often tell me that, while they don't have major problems, they're not happy in their relationships because they don't feel connected to their partners. Things are mostly good on the surface, despite some occasional bickering, but they're lonely and not sure what to do about it. This is what they're coming to therapy to change. Most of the time, they feel disconnected because they're stuck in the avoidance trap but don't know it. Just like Grace, these women have to come to understand *why* they're avoiding conflict, so they can harness its potential for deeper connection.

The Bickering Loop

At this point you might be saying, "Colette, isn't bickering part of conflict? Isn't that what we're supposed to aim for?"

In fact, no. Bickering doesn't help address the big issues in your relationship. Instead, it's number nine of the top ten avoidant coping strategies you learned about in Chapter 1. Bickering is particularly pernicious, as it erodes connection over time. There is a big difference between healthy conflict and destructive conflict, as we'll explore later, and bickering falls into the latter bucket.

Many couples are just like Grace and Andrew—getting stuck on nothingburger issues, rather than affairs or life-changing crises. Instead, it's the spats about the unwashed dishes, the backseat driving, the short retort at the end of the workday, that pull couples into bickering loops—patterns of avoidance in which couples get stuck on the surface-level problem and miss the opportunity to communicate about what's underneath it—the feelings, longings, and fears that really matter.

When you bicker, you get trapped in a back-and-forth volley of protective reactions and counterreactions that I think of like a Ping-Pong game. Each partner takes a shot at the other—a little criticism sent in one direction, some defensiveness lobbed back in return. It's relatively light at face value, just like that tiny white ball that doesn't hurt much if it hits you when it comes over the net. But over time, those wounds accumulate into larger injuries and lasting grievances.

So why do we bicker? Couples *think* they're bickering because they have differences that are preventing them from solving the problem, but what they don't realize is that most of their problems aren't solvable anyway. They involve things like differences in spending habits, desire for physical touch and intimacy, religion, needs for alone time, or even preferences in parenting styles—conflicts that don't get solved as much as endured. Psychologist Dr. John Gottman's groundbreaking longitudinal research on couples found that 69 percent of a couple's problems are unsolvable, and that most will continue to argue about the same things, over and over again, throughout their lives. Some of my couples look horrified when I quote this statistic! But here's the good news: These perpetual differences don't have to interfere with a relationship's longevity. If you can safely discuss conflicts and work through them as a team, you can actually strengthen your connection.

Couples don't break up because they have problems; they break up because they avoid them.

At the same time, these bickering loops are always about more than the issue at hand. Even the tiniest of ruptures conceal deeper roots of hurt, fear, and insecurity that will fester and grow if couples don't learn how to recognize and communicate about them. When Grace and Andrew came into my office, they didn't see how these deeper elements were playing out underneath their bickering loop, driving them to avoid conflict and grow more distant and disconnected with time.

"I'm Walking on Eggshells."

Grace and Andrew are both intelligent, well-educated doctors who told me that rationally and intellectually they already knew it wasn't healthy to avoid conflict. So why were they doing it anyway?

To understand, let's look at what was going on in their dynamic.

Grace shared that often Andrew didn't take the initiative to help at home. Maybe he didn't realize it, she reasoned, but it still left her feeling overwhelmed and alone. She didn't want to have to ask for his help on things that seemed obvious. And besides, when she did ask, he usually did it wrong anyway. If she pointed it out, he immediately got defensive or minimized her concerns. Sometimes he just flat-out ignored her, which was incredibly frustrating. It was easier just to do it herself.

Andrew worked long hours at the hospital, often overnight, but tried to contribute at home and felt like he did more than his fair share. His demanding work schedule meant he often slept in, leaving the brunt of the morning routine to his wife. Grace had to rise early and get dressed professionally, as well as wake and feed the kids and get them off to school. She had been in hyper-independence mode, trying to stay on top of everything—the kids and their activities at school and her patients and staff members at work, leaving little time for herself. Even though they had a nanny, Grace felt like the engine of the ship; she worried that if she eased up for a moment, everything would fall apart.

She had tried to get Andrew to help with the morning tasks, but her complaints seemed only to frustrate him, so she suppressed her feelings and gave up. Sometimes she found herself silently cursing out Andrew as she darted around multitasking while he snored away. It just didn't seem worth it to say anything because she didn't want to upset him, and nothing ever seemed to change anyway. Even though Grace was steaming mad at the start of the day, she bit her tongue, and by the evening it was mostly forgotten, until it started all over the next day. She wasn't processing her feelings and needs or communicating them in a constructive way and had started living in the cave of resentment. It's no surprise she wasn't feeling connected.

For his part, Andrew said he felt like his wife "had a wall up around her" and seemed perpetually annoyed with him for reasons that remained elusive. He felt like he was a great husband and father and had no idea what to do about his wife's seeming dissatisfaction. He didn't want to make her mad, and sometimes it felt like he couldn't do anything right. Andrew was always worried about doing or saying the wrong thing, so as a result, he usually did and said nothing.

When they began couples therapy, the gulf of disconnection between them had grown wider and wider from all the confusion they were perpetuating with their avoidant behaviors. Indeed, they were running several of the top ten avoidant coping strategies that you learned about in Chapter 1. They had been outsourcing their needs for emotional connection by focusing most of their energy on their kids. The little free time they had for the relationship was spent socializing with other couples or in parallel, disconnected pursuits. Most evenings,

Grace would help the kids with homework while Andrew was in the study on his computer, or vice versa. When they did come together they'd watch TV side by side, scrolling on their phones, barely talking, before collapsing into bed exhausted.

And those "petty little squabbles" Grace had referred to in their first session were repetitive bickering loops that obscured opportunities for connection.

In therapy, we examined one such instance to illuminate the why and begin to create change. Grace explained her perspective on a small exchange that she had written off as no big deal at the time.

"I asked him why he left Kai's lacrosse bag in the hall closet with all the dirty clothes in it. It stank up the entire house; I couldn't believe he just threw it in there. I just asked a simple question, and he immediately got defensive."

On the other side of the couch, Andrew sat with his arms crossed, his mouth set in a tight line. He listened, shaking his head almost imperceptibly, as if to say, *That's not what happened*, and then blurted out: "I was just trying to explain why I left it there. All I did was say, 'Get off my back for a sec, there's a perfectly good reason I left the damn bag in the closet!'" Andrew's defensiveness had begun to show itself in session.

"See?" Grace plowed on. "It's exasperating. When I get that reaction, I just can't believe it. It's so childish."

"I get it," I interjected. "And when you're feeling exasperated, what do you do next?"

"I tell him this is ridiculous. I can't communicate with you when you act like this." Grace's voice was getting more and more elevated with each question.

When I turned back to Andrew, he shared that he felt attacked when Grace reacted by criticizing him and yelling, just as she was doing in session. He would then shut down and pull away. Then Grace, feeling even more hurt and frustrated, would respond by shutting down and pulling away, too. They were both creating the very distance and disconnection they were so desperate to avoid.

"I feel like I'm walking on eggshells and can't say anything," Grace added, her voice catching. "I should be able to ask him about a bag of smelly clothes, but I can't even do that. In those moments, I don't feel like I have a partner. I want to communicate, but I can't. He leaves me no choice."

This is Grace's biggest mistake: thinking she couldn't communicate because of Andrew's reaction. While she can't control how Andrew responds, she can always choose to speak up in service of her feelings and needs rather than abandoning herself and relinquishing her power.

The Bad-Communication Report Card

I felt for Grace. She was experiencing some of the most common disconnecting responses women report receiving from their partners that I collectively refer to as **the bad-communication report card: 3 Ds and an F.** Those poor grades stand for defensiveness, dismissiveness, distancing, and fixing, which are avoidant micro moves that look like the following:

- **Defensiveness:** Your partner makes excuses and explains why they did what they did instead of listening and taking responsibility. For example, you say, "Please remember to turn off the lights when you leave the house," and your partner responds, in an exasperated tone, "I always turn them off, I just didn't today because I was in a hurry to get to work!"

- **Dismissiveness:** Your partner acts like what you're upset about is no big deal, the problem isn't really a problem, or you're making a problem out of nothing and shouldn't be upset in the first place. For example, you ask, "Could you please text me if you're going to stay out late?" and your partner responds, "Relax, you always know where I am, there's nothing to get so worked up about."

- **Distancing:** Your partner pulls away, shuts down, and retreats instead of staying engaged and talking things through. For example, your feelings are hurt and you start crying. Your partner responds with an uncomfortable blank stare and exits the conversation—and the room as quickly as possible.

- **Fixing:** Your partner tries to solve the problem or give advice rather than tuning in and connecting to you emotionally. For example, after a tough day at work, you're venting: "I'm so sick of getting piled on at work, sometimes I just want to quit!" All you wanted was a listening ear, but your partner responds by jumping in with "Whoa, you can't quit! You just need to get to work a little earlier and write your boss an email about what you have on your plate. That's a much better way to handle it."

These responses are hurtful, confusing, invalidating, and, of course, disconnecting. If you've been on the receiving end of some bad-communication report card action, then you've experienced firsthand how much it can make you want to pull your hair out and give up on trying to be heard. I know because I've been there. If you haven't, good for you; you're one of the few lucky ones.

Bad-communication report card responses are very common, particularly with men, thanks to rampant socialization that has finally begun to change. For years, men were raised to present a tough veneer. They were allowed to show only two affect states: stoic or angry. Yet men experience the same range of emotions as women, despite being conditioned to disconnect from their feelings and dismiss them altogether. Is it any surprise, then, that they do this to their partners?

But for people of all genders, bad-communication report card responses tend to be the automatic defense mechanisms for those who are uncomfortable with emotion. Usually the partner reacting with defensiveness, dismissiveness, distancing, and fixing is interpreting their partner's communication as a statement of some combination of the following:

- You're in trouble.
- You're a disappointment.
- You're failing.
- You're not good enough.

These responses are unconscious attempts to deflect with logic and avoid feelings of shame, inadequacy, and helplessness. But they cut off connection and leave the other person feeling stymied and alone with their feelings.

Most of the time all we really want is to be heard and understood. Another client of mine put it beautifully when she explained why she didn't want a problem-solving response from her partner and what she longed for instead. "When I'm down in a tunnel with my feelings, I don't want you to dig me out. I want you to crawl in there with me, put up a tent, and camp out beside me."

That's it. *Hear me and be with me in what I'm feeling.* Yet so many people simply don't know how to do this. They're not comfortable sitting with emotion and have learned that they're responsible for people's feelings, especially their partner's, and must do something actionable to help. If they can't make their partner feel better, then they're letting them down. Thus, they react quickly and without forethought to resolve their discomfort by getting defensive, dismissing what their partner is saying, distancing themselves from the conversation, jumping right into trying to fix the problem, or a combination of all four. Some counterblame, saying things like, "Well, you do this, too," which is another form of defensiveness. Until they learn to connect with and explore their inner world, those engaging in bad-communication report card responses are rarely aware of the shame and pain that drives these reactions.

In therapy, Andrew discovered that he got defensive because he felt like he could never get it right for her. His defensiveness prevented him from feeling the shame of failure, but while unintended, it also sent a message to Grace that it wasn't safe to communicate and left her feeling invalidated and thwarted.

At first it was difficult for Grace to understand how in the world he could take her communication as an indication of failure. She did not attack him; she simply asked why a bag of dirty clothes with a nasty odor was left to stagnate in the closet. At this stage, before the couple have learned more about the deeper mechanisms at play, it's difficult for Grace to comprehend how or why Andrew could have taken her question that way.

Grace shared that when Andrew was defensive, the message she got was that they're not a team, she doesn't have a partner, and she's alone in it. That didn't represent how she felt globally in the relationship, but it was the message she received *in those moments*. Grace felt frustrated, hurt, and disappointed but didn't articulate those feelings in a clear and gentle way. Instead, she reacted by criticizing him for getting defensive and then retreating in silence. She didn't see that this was a choice that landed her squarely in the avoidance trap.

Like Grace, many clients tell me they want to communicate but that they can't because it doesn't go well. They believe their silence isn't self-imposed but rather inflicted upon them by their partners. It's their partner's fault they can't speak up, and they would if they could. They get those bad-communication report card responses that shut them down, or they don't want to hurt their partners. Of course none of us wants to hurt the person we love, but usually our actions aren't entirely altruistic. Rather than staying quiet to spare a loved one's feelings, the true motivation is to avoid the anxiety and discomfort *we* feel inside when our partner is upset.

Let's face it: Most of us are not comfortable with conflict at all. Our good-girl conditioning kicks in, as we've been raised to be selfless and taught to take responsibility for other people's feelings. People-pleasing comes from fear of losing approval and being judged, and when it comes to our partners, the fear can be even more powerful. It can feel downright wrong, if not dangerous, to upset someone, especially your partner.

We avoid saying what needs to be said because we can't tolerate our partner's displeasure. It's not really about being nice; it's about not wanting to feel bad. We're avoiding emotions we don't want to experience. It's easier to skate on past the hard thing than it is to stop and sit in something unpleasant. But if we want intimacy and we want to live resentment-free, then we have to.

Speaking up in our intimate relationships means that we will inevitably upset, disappoint, and anger our partners. We have to normalize that it is okay to upset others by voicing our truth, and it is not our job to rescue our partners from their painful feelings.

Part of what shut Grace down was seeing Andrew get upset, which was massively uncomfortable for her. She didn't realize that she was really trying to avoid the discomfort and painful feelings that conflict brought up for her. She believed that Andrew's responses made it impossible for her to communicate, and this justified the choice to avoid. While I empathized with her plight, and even related to it myself, as a therapist I knew that she would have to recognize her role in creating this dilemma—that she was criticizing and then going quiet—and start asserting herself. She had the power for healthy self-expression inside her; she just hadn't learned to channel it yet.

Bad-communication report card responses are painful, but they don't have to lead to cycles of reactivity and disconnection. Grace can't control what Andrew does, but when she puts down her Ping-Pong paddle and chooses an intentional response, she has the power to change the game.

In the bickering loop, all Andrew gets from her is mild criticism, a look of displeasure, and a cold shoulder. Her reactions only confirm what he's already fearing inside—he's a disappointment to her. He then responds to her silent retreat with a withdrawal of his own. His reactions only confirm what she's already fearing inside—she doesn't have a partner and is all alone. In the moment, the behaviors they show each other on the outside confirm the worst fears they have on the inside.

When they began therapy, Grace and Andrew didn't understand why they were stuck or how to get out of it. Their relationship seemed secure on the outside—they were financially well off, no one wanted a divorce, and there were no concerns about affairs. But underneath that surface-level security, the relationship was much more insecure than they realized. The irony is that these avoidant coping strategies were making the relationship *less* secure over time. These strategies were creating a much bigger problem than the smelly lacrosse clothes.

Many people with relationship struggles don't have big problems to deal with, yet they're still stuck in painful patterns of disconnection that can destroy their relationships. Bickering loops come in many different flavors. Perhaps you tend to go quiet immediately, or you go back and forth trying to prove your point and decide who's right, or maybe you make earnest attempts to resolve things and then disengage when it doesn't seem to land. Perhaps you don't even bicker but altogether avoid any discussion that could be contentious.

Whatever version you experience when you and your partner get stuck like this, these automated impulses—to criticize, defend, avoid—are taking over and can do real damage if this keeps happening over time.

There are much deeper forces at play that drive these reactions and explain why conflict is so scary and complicated. When you understand what's happening on an attachment level and in your nervous system instead of allowing these reactions to hijack your relationship, you can override your automated impulses, address conflict constructively, and create the lasting connection you want.

How Attachment Influences Relationships

Attachment theory is the science of relationship bonding. It holds both the answers to why couples get stuck in the avoidance trap and the solutions for getting out if it. Therefore, if we want to have more connected relationships, we need to understand the attachment forces at play.

Attachment theory explains that we are biologically wired to form close emotional bonds from birth through adulthood in order to survive and thrive. Our nervous systems are designed to generate feel-good neurochemicals such as dopamine and phenylethylamine (PEA), and bonding chemicals such as oxytocin and vasopressin. These incentivize long-term attachment by flooding us with feelings of safety and contentment in relationships.

On the flip side, loneliness kills. Research from the landmark Harvard Study of Adult Development has shown that social isolation has a higher morbidity than obesity and smoking. According to the Centers for Disease Control and Prevention (CDC), it significantly increases the risk of death from all causes, and in people with heart failure, the risk of death goes up nearly fourfold. It isn't just physical, either; loneliness leads to depression and anxiety and a host of other mental health concerns. This may shock you, but when we examine it through the lens of attachment, it makes perfect sense.

Building on the work of British psychiatrist and psychologist Dr. John Bowlby, world-renowned psychologist Dr. Sue Johnson identified that we all need responsiveness, security, and comfort from a reliable loved one "from the cradle to the grave." Johnson developed a model of couples therapy called Emotionally Focused Therapy (EFT), which is based on attachment science and has become the gold standard in evidence-based treatment. This model helps couples identify and de-escalate what she calls *negative cycles*—stuck interactional patterns such as bickering loops—and strengthen their bonds through sharing and responding to emotional needs. It's essential to know that our partners will be there for us with comfort, support, and reassurance.

Attachment theory helps us understand why breakups are so devastating; why we struggle to end relationships even when we've outgrown them; why abandonment and rejection can feel like death. Once we're attached, it's hard to let go—and the seeds of origin for our attachment patterns lie in our early childhood conditioning.

Attachment in Childhood

In adulthood, though we can take care of our own basic needs, we still depend on close, connected loved ones (like our romantic partners) to support us emotionally. That need for emotional connection starts early—in childhood. At this early stage in life we also need a caretaker to meet not just our basic physical needs but, crucially, our emotional ones, too. For kids, secure attachment can literally be a life-or-death proposition, and what we're realizing now is that the attachment patterns we form early in childhood have profound implications for the relationships we form later in life.

Early childhood developmental experiences leave an imprint, creating either healthy or unhealthy ways of coping. Children who are well cared for emotionally tend to learn the two healthiest coping mechanisms: (1) to express their emotions freely, and (2) to turn to trusted loved ones for comfort and support. When children don't have reliable adults who respond to them consistently, they develop other (often less productive) coping strategies to manage distress, like withdrawing from connection when upset, disconnecting from their feelings, and self-soothing with activities—such as reading, watching television, or playing video games—or substances—such as tobacco, alcohol, and marijuana. In fact, it is often in childhood that the roots of addiction take hold. For example, sex addiction can start with using porn to feel better during the preteen years; compulsive eating may begin with a need for escape in a contentious home; alcohol can become the go-to mood regulator or social lubricant in early teenage years. Then when these children grow up, these same tactics are brought into their adult relationships as well.

Dr. John Bowlby pioneered the importance of childhood attachment. His research showed that children experienced distress when separated from primary caretakers that manifested in protest, despair, or detachment. He found that children develop inner-working models—core beliefs about themselves—based on their relationships with their primary caretakers. For example, when mothers were consistently engaged and responsive, children developed a sense of confidence—a belief that they are valuable, worthy, and deserving of care. Conversely, when children did not receive steady, responsive care, they developed a sense of insecurity. They came to see themselves as unlovable, unworthy, or undeserving of fundamental care.

Feeling secure or insecure in these early caregiver relationships leads to the development of an attachment style—an inner template for ways of behaving and managing closeness in relationships. There are three primary attachment styles—the first being healthy and secure, and the second two reflecting unhealthy and insecure attachment in childhood:

- **Secure attachment:** Children who are secure believe that they are worthy of love and care and can count on receiving it. At least one consistently nurturing relationship with an adult is typically needed to form this secure style. These children don't see separation from caregivers as potential abandonment or rejection; they are confident that when parents leave they will return and, therefore, feel safe enough to engage in independent play. Secure children are open about their feelings and comfortable being close to others. They see caregivers as a secure base in the world and trust they can go to them when needed for comfort and support. Their credo is "I know you'll be here when I need you."

- **Anxious attachment:** An anxious style reflects insecure attachment. This style may develop in childhood when caretaking adults are inconsistent, unavailable, or unreliable. As a result, children who are anxiously attached may be preoccupied with their caregivers and fearful of abandonment. These children develop inner-working models of believing they are unlovable or undeserving of care. To protect themselves from potential abandonment, they may protest separation, cling, cry, and seek constant proximity to their adult caregivers. Their credo is "If you leave me, I'm afraid you'll never come back."

- **Avoidant attachment:** This style also reflects insecure attachment and may develop when early caregivers are inconsistent, unavailable, or unreliable. Because they lack predictable care, children with an avoidant style fear rejection and protect themselves with undue self-reliance. They have inner-working models of being unworthy, flawed, and not good enough. Avoidant children don't turn to caregivers or trust them to be there, so they tend to withdraw when distressed. They prefer to handle things on their own and soothe themselves with distractions rather than seeking comfort and connection with loved ones. Their credo is "If I don't need you, you can't ever disappoint me."

Experts initially believed that your attachment style remained fixed over the course of your life. But we now know that attachment styles can be shaped by our relationships *throughout* our lifespan. This is good news: Even if you didn't experience secure attachment as a child, you can develop secure attachment in adulthood! Nonetheless, early childhood attachment experiences undoubtedly leave an imprint on how children grow up and connect as adults.

Secure versus Insecure Attachment in Childhood

If we understand the influence of our childhood attachment patterns, then we can make more conscious choices toward secure attachment in our adult relationships. Let's take a look at the difference between secure and insecure attachment styles with two very different kids on the same playground.

Jessica is a loving, caring mom who is regularly available to four-year-old Brady. She looks her in the eye, is physically affectionate, reads to her, comforts her when she's scared, and tucks her in at night. When Brady cries out for Mom because she had a bad dream, Jessica runs in and sits with her, rubbing her back and soothing her fears until she falls back asleep. When Brady cries because she drops her cup and spills her milk, Mom comforts her and validates her experience, reflecting that it's okay that she's sad and it's okay to make a mistake. Brady eventually stops crying and resumes playing. Because of this responsiveness, Brady is securely attached. When she and Mom go to the park, Brady plays with the other kids while Jessica sits chatting with the other mothers. Occasionally Brady pops over to share her playground successes, excited that she made it all the way across the monkey bars. Jessica claps and praises her while Brady runs to rejoin the children. She is confident that Mom will be there if she needs her.

In contrast, let's look at Billy and the type of environment that creates a more insecurely attached child, in this case, the anxious attachment style.

Alison is a distracted and stressed mom who is not emotionally available to her four-year-old son, Billy. She yells at him when frustrated, gets irritated when he's upset, and is often busy on her phone. When he drops his cup and spills milk, she screams at him for being careless and leaves him alone to cry. She does not help him make sense of his feelings or comfort him when he is sad and scared. Because of this, when Alison takes Billy to the park, he's anxious and afraid to leave her side. He's reluctant to play for fear that he'll make a mistake that angers Mom. He sits by her side and watches Brady and the other kids on the monkey bars, while Mom talks on the phone and ignores him. He'd like to join them, but he's too preoccupied with Mom for carefree play. Alison scolds him for not playing and tells him he's acting like a baby, which makes him feel even worse about himself.

Does either of these scenarios sound familiar to you?

Many people fall somewhere between Billy's and Brady's childhood experiences. Some clients tell me that they had a great childhood and knew they were loved. Yet a closer examination reveals that there was actually little emotional support, and their caretakers didn't help them learn to manage their feelings. If you're over forty this may be particularly true. Like me, you might have grown up roaming the neighborhood with your friends from dawn to dusk like a pack of wolves. This was a wonderful aspect of my generation's upbringing that has been lost in this era. Because of both safety concerns and cultural shifts in parenting, it has become the norm to closely monitor kids.

In previous generations, it was not uncommon to take a more hands-off approach. Part of this was instilling kids with a pull-yourself-up-by-the-bootstraps mentality. Many were raised to shrug off adversity and get back out there, and the ability to do so was seen as a sign of strength. What was also commonplace was to ignore and minimize emotional experiences. Being emotional was often misinterpreted as a sign of weakness rather than as a healthy connection to one's internal physiological and psychological experience. Back then, the expectation was that you would deal with your feelings on your own. This was part of the ethos of rugged American individualism, which perpetuated the false but widely accepted idea that we don't need anyone but ourselves. Attachment science has proven otherwise.

We now know that human beings are herd animals designed to live in close proximity and connection with loved ones. Not only is this optimal, but it's necessary for survival—both physically and emotionally.

In my own early life, I was fortunate to have parents who were emotionally available and responsive. My brother wasn't born until I was nearly ten years old, so my mom and dad and I were a tight-knit little threesome who did everything together. At five years old, I was obsessed with Nancy Drew books and my parents would read the mysteries out loud with me, helping me with the big words so that I grasped every bit of the spunky red headed sleuth's exploits. As a sensitive, imaginative child, I had frequent nightmares and would invade their room with my sleeping bag, finding respite on the floor at the foot of their bed. I felt as loved, safe, and secure as possible—something every child deserves and far too many are denied.

My halcyon childhood came to a screeching halt when I was eleven years old. My parents' marriage blew up, seemingly overnight, and suddenly the atmosphere was filled with tension and anger. My parents, who had been so loving and attentive, were suddenly stressed and preoccupied. No one focused on my emotional needs anymore. I was scared and struggled to cope with the confusing changes on my own, escaping into books and stories I conjured up in my head, while trying to adjust to the turbulence of middle school, not the easiest time for most young girls. Nobody acknowledged what was happening at home, but I knew it in my bones—my family was falling apart. I had to grow up fast and become the emotional adult I needed.

There were episodes of fighting and separating that were hard on me. I coped by smoking cigarettes, venting to my friends, and acting the contrarian at school. While this unsettling period had a lasting impact on me, the solid foundation of my younger years went a long way toward creating secure attachment and a strong sense of self. Based on my parents' early consistent care, I developed a core belief that I am worthy and deserving of love. However, the arguing in later years led to insecurity and a more anxiously attached style in my early romantic relationships that I had to overcome as an adult.

EXPLORING YOUR CHILDHOOD ATTACHMENT

Let's explore *your* childhood experiences so you can reflect on what you learned about attachment and coping strategies.

Warning: If your childhood was a time of great trauma, this exercise may activate feelings that can flood and overwhelm you. Perhaps it's too painful to revisit this time, and you don't feel comfortable. Please use your discretion as to what you can tolerate and proceed accordingly.

If you have a photo of yourself as a child it might be helpful to take a look at it to evoke your memory. If you don't have a picture handy, no worries; just allow your mind to access whatever it can without forcing anything. Everyone is different in terms of how far back they can remember, so just go with whatever comes up for you. There are no right or wrong answers.

You may want to read through the following description and questions before going through the exercise. Have paper or your journal ready, so you can answer the questions and make notes.

Now close your eyes and take a few deep, cleansing breaths so you can relax and orient yourself to the present moment. Once you've settled in, gently float back and begin to visualize your younger self. Take the time and allow space for any and all mental images and sensations that arise to present themselves to you. As you sit with your experience, consider the following questions:

- What do you notice about that time?

- Can you see yourself with your parent(s) or caregiver(s)?

- How did you feel when you were a child?

- Were you relaxed or filled with fear and tension?

- How did your primary caretakers respond to you?

- What were your childhood experiences like overall?

When you're ready, come back to the room and take a few deep breaths to get grounded. Then write out your answers to the following questions: These questions are adapted from George, Kaplan, and Main's Adult Attachment Interview, which is a series of questions that therapists ask to better understand clients' attachment history and how it may affect their current relationships.

1. What was happening in your family dynamic when you were a child?

2. Was there someone who spent a lot of time with you? Were they focused and present—not just in terms of being there physically, but in really talking with you, looking you in the eye, and listening? Was there someone who made you feel important and special?

3. If so, how did that person show you that you mattered? Did they hug you, spend quality time with you, or offer praise and words of affirmation?

4. Did someone comfort you when you were scared? How did they comfort you?

5. If not, how did you learn to comfort and soothe yourself? Did you go to a trusted adult or handle things on your own? Like many kids, did you seek solace in distractions such as reading, TV, junk food, writing, sports, pornography, cigarettes, drugs, alcohol, or something else?

6. What did you observe in your parents' marriage? Did they speak to each other respectfully (for example, hug, kiss, fight, and then make up)? Did they avoid conflict altogether? Did they seem happy but somewhat disconnected? Or did they fight and triangulate, bringing you into their tension inappropriately?

7. Was there abuse in your home? Physical? Mental? Emotional? How did you see your mom, dad, or primary caretaker soothing themself? Did they turn to substances, affairs, or other distractions? Did you sit at the dinner table together as a family or occupy your own little silos?

8. How were emotions handled in your household? Were they expressed or repressed? Did you learn to suppress and avoid uncomfortable feelings? Is that what your parents or primary caretakers did?

Make note of anything else important that came up for you. It may be helpful to refer back to these discoveries as you're working through subsequent exercises in the book.

Attachment Style in Adulthood

Talking about your childhood attachment style is *not* intended to blame your parents for events in the past! By examining what was modeled for you in your family of origin and how you were taught to manage comfort and distress, you can start to understand how all this influenced your attachment behaviors in adulthood. With awareness you can learn to make more conscious and intentional choices in how you communicate—choices that allow you to stop avoidant behavior and instead move the needle toward connected, secure attachment.

Let's go back to Grace and Andrew, our avoidant couple from the beginning of this chapter, for a moment and take a look at how their childhoods influenced their avoidant patterns of behavior before they learned healthier ways to interact.

Young Grace's parents were both first-generation Korean immigrants who were kept busy running the family pharmacy—Grace knew she was loved but always had the feeling they "didn't have much time for her." Grace reported that her childhood experiences were mostly positive, but her parents were not demonstrative. There were high expectations; her parents made it clear that she would become a doctor, and they would settle for nothing less. She complied and strove to be the best. Grace often felt alone, although she didn't recognize it as such at the time. No one really tended to her emotionally or helped her learn how to make sense of her feelings. Therefore, she learned to tune them out and carry on. This bled into adulthood, leading her to react to Andrew's defensiveness by quickly disengaging.

Furthermore, her parents mostly avoided conflict but would occasionally blow up in a nasty fight. Grace would hide in her room, listening to her mother hurl insults at her father. The rest of the time her mother said little. She would come to Grace and complain about her father, instead of directly addressing her grievances with him, which wasn't healthy for her marriage or fair to Grace. All of this left Grace feeling terrified of conflict and reluctant to engage in it.

Andrew had a very different experience. His parents were totally emotionally disconnected. He didn't witness any fighting, but he didn't witness any bonding or affection, either. They parented him in a similar fashion and used tough love, the method they were raised with and believed was best. His parents also had high expectations, which they demonstrated in different ways. Mom would tell him even an A– was unacceptable, while Dad would punish him with a belt for a subpar performance. When he was upset, he would retreat to his sanctuary in their finished basement. He built model cars at his workbench, pushing his feelings aside to focus on his creations. His parents were trying to help him toughen up and be his best, but what their behavior taught him was how to disconnect from his feelings and manage them on his own. This adaptive response protected him from feeling the pain of judgment from his parents. Deep down he developed a sense of inadequacy that fueled his defensiveness with Grace.

For both of them, all of what they witnessed and experienced in childhood influenced how they showed up in their bickering loop and why they got stuck in the avoidance trap. They were children without reliable adults to respond to them with care, help them make sense of their feelings, and provide comfort in times of distress. As a result, they developed compensatory strategies to cope that they carried into adulthood. Instead of openly sharing feelings and asking for their emotional needs to be met, they avoided vulnerable self-disclosure and protected themselves. They didn't know how to do what they had never seen or heard. Their avoidance meant less discomfort in the moment but, unfortunately, also less connection and closeness over time.

Avoidant Behavior as a Survival Strategy

When we avoid conflict, we're trying to shield ourselves from pain and protect our relationships from damage and destruction. Conflict feels fraught with the potential to jeopardize our relationships and cause pain, and we are naturally averse to both. Avoidance is an instinctive but misguided survival strategy: In an effort to protect ourselves and our relationships, our nervous systems prioritize protection and short-term comfort over the long-term potential for growth and connection that comes from confronting the issue and handling conflict well.

Let's dig in and take a look at these deeper forces—both the desire to avoid pain and the desire to protect our relationships—that compel us to avoid.

The Natural Desire to Avoid Pain

To the nervous system, comfort is coded as safety, and conflict is coded as a dangerous harbinger of pain. Therefore, it's natural and instinctual to want to avoid conflict for our own protection.

In some ways embracing conflict for growth is like telling your brain that you should put your hand on the stove when you're pretty sure it's too hot to touch. All of your instincts are screaming, *No, danger, danger, danger!* Then you touch it anyway, and a funny thing happens. It turns out that it's only slightly warm to the touch. Much like this metaphor, we're afraid to embrace conflict because we think we're going to get burned, even though it's usually not as bad as we expect it to be.

When you've been burned in the past around conflict, it's even harder to take the risk. The brain and nervous system hold on to *everything* bad that has ever happened to try to keep us alert and aware, so that if a similar threat is presented we don't get hurt again. We all suffer from past relationship hurts, some that haven't fully healed and some that have left scars. Our hypervigilant brains will not let us forget those hurts for our own protection, but this can hold us back when it comes to healthy communication.

The Natural Desire to Protect the Relationship

Not only are we trying to protect ourselves from pain, but when we avoid conflict we're also trying to protect our relationships from damage and disconnection.

Adult attachment styles can influence how we attempt to protect our relationships. You learned coping mechanisms for self-protection, emotional regulation, safety, and connection in childhood. You developed parts of yourself to cope with distress as an adaptation to your environment that you may now use to protect your relationship. If adults failed to provide you with a loving, engaged presence in childhood, you may not know that responding with emotional attunement is something that's desirable or needed in adult relationships. It's hard to handle conflict in a way that you never knew existed. Often partners have to learn emotional connection together in adulthood, for the very first time.

But as you get older, you're also greatly influenced by your peer and romantic relationships, so in adulthood your predominant attachment style is most likely the result of a combination of your childhood experiences and these subsequent forces.

Here's how the three primary attachment styles may manifest in your adult relationships:

- **Secure attachment:** Secure adults see themselves as lovable and worthy, feel fundamentally safe in their relationships, and invest in intimacy and closeness. They can regulate and share their emotions and seek comfort from their partners. An adult with this style sees their relationship as a secure base to return to in times of distress and a means for coping with life's ups and downs. They are less likely to see conflict as a threat and more willing to engage in it and give their partners the benefit of the doubt. Secure adults are comfortable with both individual autonomy and close connection and don't see them as mutually exclusive. Their credo is "We are unique individuals who do best when we function as a closely connected team."

- **Anxious attachment:** Those with this style lack confidence in their relationships and don't trust their partners to be there for them. They may believe their partners don't really love or appreciate them and are as terrified of abandonment as anxiously attached children. These individuals want to share their emotions but may struggle to regulate their feelings without active support. They are preoccupied with their partners and need them to provide a great deal of external reassurance. Those with an anxious style may be hypersensitive to any hint of distance and seek to control and maintain close proximity to their partners. They perceive conflict as a threat and want to resolve it immediately to alleviate their acute distress. Their credo is "I could lose you at any moment, so I feel safe only when you're right beside me and we're good."

- **Avoidant attachment:** Adults with this predominant style don't feel confident that they can count on their partners, or anybody else for that matter, and keep people at a distance. Deep down, avoidant adults see themselves as deficient or defective and fear rejection. They remain detached as protection from it. They seek control instead of closeness and do not feel comfortable sharing their emotions. Avoidantly attached adults see intimacy as suffocating and vulnerability as weakness, and therefore they tend to compartmentalize and disconnect from feelings. They perceive any conflict as a threat to their relationship and feel safest coping on their own, so they pull away, shut down, or withdraw. These individuals pride themselves on their independence, and rather than turning to their partners, they may seek comfort in distractions or activities, even those that are self-destructive. Their credo is "If I keep you at a distance, you can't hurt me."

If your partner is unreliable and inconsistent in delivering emotional support, you may lean more toward the insecure end of the spectrum in that relationship, regardless of your childhood attachment style. The good news: These styles are not fixed! Most of us are on a spectrum that can fluctuate, and we may be more secure in some relationships and less secure in others. It's never too late to learn how to connect emotionally and move toward secure attachment in your relationship. Even if you're securely attached in your romantic relationship, you will still be sensitive because it's part of the human condition—we're wired for attachment and naturally predisposed to avoid anything that feels like a threat.

Attachment Fears, Attachment Threats

When you love someone, the thought of losing them can strike a chord of terror into even the hardest heart. It's no surprise that crimes of passion occur when someone is spurned. The neurochemical forces of attachment are deeply embedded in the human nervous system, creating potent cocktails that keep us hooked, committed, and fiercely protective of our bonds. Attachment is what makes it so hard to end a relationship, even when it's long past its expiration date. Deep down we're all afraid of rejection and abandonment, which feel like death. The suffering generated by these events is experienced as intensely as physical pain and in fact lights up the same regions of the brain, looking eerily similar on PET imaging scans. Research has found that heartbreak is so powerful it can even diminish your IQ.

Thus, the fear looms large that we will do or say something that creates a rift and jeopardizes our all-important bond. If an interaction seems like it could devolve into an argument, fears that sound like bursts of wisdom can pop up in your mind like fireworks, pulling you to avoid or disengage. Your inner voice starts warning you to self-silence, telling you that it is no longer safe to communicate. This part of you is trying to help you protect your relationship from harm, but in an effort to do so, it can cause you to self-abandon by not expressing what needs to be said, both for yourself and for the relationship.

Here are some of the most common warning messages women say

to themselves that are generated by fear and designed to halt communication to protect the relationship:

- *I'd better stop because I might say something hurtful.*
- *I'll make my partner angry if I continue.*
- *If I keep talking, this will escalate and we'll get in a fight.*

Do you notice an inner dialogue like this in a difficult moment? You may be aware of such trepidations, but have you thought about why these thoughts feel so scary? If you say something hurtful, or make your partner angry, or cause a disagreement to escalate, then not only would it be uncomfortable but also, on an attachment level, it could mean the demise of your relationship.

Underneath most of our interactions are deep-seated, often unconscious attachment fears of rejection, abandonment, and losing the one we love. It's impossible to overstate how enormous yet submerged these fears are. I think of them like blue whales—the biggest creatures in the ocean, omnipresent but invisible. If you're out kayaking in the Pacific, enjoying the crystal-blue water and tropical scenery, it's easy to forget what lurks out of sight miles down—a giant three-hundred-thousand-pound whale with a heart the size of a car that could breach out of the water at any moment from right underneath you.

It's much the same in our relationships. We don't realize that the biggest thing is what's hidden and swimming down deep. Our attachment fears are the most powerful forces at play, and they impact everything that happens on the surface in our interactions.

We will do anything to prevent rejection and abandonment in our primary romantic relationships. This makes us hypervigilant to everything that could imperil them. Even if we had a securely attached childhood, because of our natural wiring and the importance of these close bonds to our survival, we easily perceive the smallest verbal or nonverbal cues from our partners as threats to the relationship and engage in avoidant behaviors. These threats are what I call **attachment bombs**—signals from our partner that alert us to impending danger. They can be as minor as a raised eyebrow or as intense as being yelled at; suddenly we're disconnected from our partners and our relationship seems to be in jeopardy.

Our nervous systems are also a key player in what drives us to be sensitive to these attachment bombs and dive headfirst into the avoidance trap. Neuroscientist Dr. Stephen Porges identified that we distinguish between safety and danger in an instant in a process known as neuroception. We have an internal radar that perpetually scans the environment outside our conscious awareness. It enables us to detect even subtle changes in our partner's facial expressions, body language, and vocal tones to discern threat.

Have you ever interacted with someone and gotten a bad vibe? Maybe they didn't do or say anything wrong, but you could just feel that something was off? That was your built-in radar, working to determine how safe you were on an instinctual level. This is why, when it comes to your relationship, it's less about *what* your partner says and more about *how* they're saying it.

Your partner transmits signals that send your nervous system a cue of safety or danger. In Edward Tronick's famous Still Face Experiment in the 1970s, infants became increasingly distressed when their primary caregivers responded to their attempts to engage with a blank facial expression. They reacted by amping up their attempts to get a response, then dissolving into tears, and eventually giving up and becoming despondent.

Despite how unpleasant it is to witness, the experiment shows how deeply impacted we are by the responses of our closest others. In communication, empathy registers when our partner's facial expression tracks ours. If you're distressed and your partner has a stony expression on their face or gives you no response at all, it's hurtful and confusing. Therefore, when you see your partner's face go cold, that's an attachment bomb right there, alerting your body to danger.

Often the things we receive as attachment bombs are based on past hurts that haven't healed. When an attachment bomb goes off in a relationship, the limbic system, the part of the brain that regulates emotion and memory, detects this instantaneously and perceives it as a threat. In such moments, the brain is focused on one thing only—survival.

It's an evolutionary adaptation from prehistoric times. If a predator jumped out to ambush you, this fight-or-flight response would allow you to instinctively determine in a nanosecond, without forethought, which response would be most likely to keep you alive. The amygdala, an important part of the limbic system, detects a threat and signals fear, as the nervous system shuts off the logic center in the prefrontal cortex. It shunts all blood, energy, and resources toward protection, flooding you with the hormones needed to fight, flee, freeze, or even fawn—an attempt to cope with danger through appeasement. If your system determines that fleeing is the best strategy, you're flooded with the adrenaline needed to run. On the other hand, if your nervous system interprets that the threat is too great and you have no chance to survive, it opts for freeze, shutting you down with as little pain as possible in preparation to die.

These prehistoric responses form the basis for what we do with our partners in a moment of attachment distress. Although they are a natural instinct, this becomes a vicious cycle for couples who trigger each other's fight-or-flight responses and get stuck in negative interactional patterns that block closeness and emotional intimacy.

In today's world, we've evolved to the point where it's rare to encounter predators in everyday life (which is why I won't go in the ocean beyond two feet deep nearly forty-five years after seeing the movie *Jaws*). "The predator" that most often activates our natural fear response is, weirdly enough, our partner. The problem is that the brain is still stuck on its original prehistoric setting. Many situations with our partners are misunderstandings, but the brain overreacts. It doesn't distinguish between what's happened in the past and what may happen in the present. Its job is to alert you to danger, so you can respond to the threat. It's better to have a false positive than a false negative, meaning that from a survival standpoint, it's preferable to assume the worst and act to avoid it than to assume the best and miss a threat and die.

The brain tells our system to panic and protect ourselves as if we are about to be eaten by Jaws, when in many modern scenarios in which we're self-protecting, the "threat" may be no more than our partner acting grouchy after a long day. While that doesn't feel good, it's not going to kill us. If we're not aware of the natural proclivities of our nervous system, we may react in ways that are more protective than what's actually warranted by the level of threat at hand. This causes a bigger problem than the original trigger.

A part of us comes out with iterations of fight, flight, freeze, or fawn survival strategies, often defaulting to ways we learned to protect in childhood when we weren't developmentally capable of being assertive. Because of our self-protective wiring and the primal importance of our attachment bonds, when small things are perceived as threats to us and our relationships, we will do anything to quell them, and much of the time that takes the form of avoidance.

From this vantage point, it makes complete sense that when we detect a threat or when something feels like it has the potential to devolve, we avoid instead of effectively communicating. When we're operating out of survival mode, our nervous system thinks we're under attack and may suffer greatly if we don't protect ourselves. In the moment, conflict seems like the enemy. Our nervous system is doing what it's designed to do—get us back to safety. The problem is that this holds us back from the adult communication we're capable of, the kind of self-expression that creates secure attachment within us and closeness and intimacy with our partners. Even though these protective avoidance strategies make sense on a nervous-system level, if we let them take over and run our interactions, they will eventually destroy the connection and fabric of goodwill in our relationships—the very thing we're trying to prevent.

How Grace and Andrew Overcame Avoidance

Now that you understand the deeper forces at play, we can reexamine Grace and Andrew's bickering loop around the dirty lacrosse clothes through the lens of attachment.

For each of them, the pattern began with the other's behavior. For Andrew, it started with what he perceived as Grace criticizing him about leaving the bag in the closet, while for Grace, it was Andrew's defensive response. Each received the other's action as a mini attachment bomb that blew up in their face.

What made Grace's "simple question" an attachment bomb was the subtle tension in her voice that Andrew's nervous system read as a cue of danger.

Andrew got defensive, a knee-jerk fight-or-flight response from his limbic brain, responding as he would if a predator jumped out of the bushes. In his nervous system, beneath conscious awareness, he registered this criticism, and what he interpreted as Grace's disappointment, as a threat to him and to their relationship.

In turn, Grace received his defensiveness as a threat to both her well-being and the sanctity of the relationship. Before doing the work to increase awareness, Grace thought she was justifiably reacting to her husband's offense. However, her nervous system told a story of predation and survival. Her silence upon encountering his defensiveness was self-protective, an attempt to prevent pain and damage to the relationship. This was motivated by a subconscious fear of jeopardizing the relationship with conflict, and a deeper fear of potential rejection and abandonment. No matter how unlikely she knew that was on a rational level, on a physiological level in her body, the threat felt all too real.

Yet this avoidant strategy didn't help her get what she really wanted and needed, which was to be heard and understood and have greater connection with her husband. Like Grace, Andrew also wasn't getting his emotional needs met. He came out of these interactions feeling like exactly what he feared was true, that he was a failure in her eyes.

When Grace and Andrew were avoiding conflict, they were in a feedback loop of protection that kept them stuck and blocked the very connection they longed for. This pattern was fueled by unconscious fears, aka "blue whales" under the surface. Some of the attachment bombs seemed petty, and it was tempting to sweep them under the rug, but by failing to acknowledge those deeper fears and confront what was important to each of them, they missed an opportunity for growth and connection. Every time they reacted protectively in their loop, they created more insecurity and doubt in the relationship, moving further away from secure attachment.

Your system is wired to detect threat quickly and automatically, but if you don't acknowledge the deeper fears and forces at play you will react with fight-or-flight responses that increase the likelihood that you'll trigger your partner in return. Because of automated survival impulses, you'll avoid something that feels like a threat and get the opposite of what you really want—connection, comfort, and getting your true attachment needs met.

For Grace this is what was happening with Andrew. She had been living in the cave of resentment, blaming Andrew for her failure to communicate. While those bad-communication report card responses from Andrew set off alarm bells that coerced her to shut down the conversation, they also offered an opportunity for her to recognize the deeper forces at work, connect to herself, and choose a more intentional response.

Throughout therapy, I helped Grace and Andrew learn to identify when they were playing toxic emotional Ping-Pong, put down their paddles, and get into a healthier communication pattern. Grace realized that she had been stuffing down her hurt and anger about feeling alone and not getting the help she needed, instead of communicating clearly. This frustration crept into her tone when she asked even seemingly innocuous questions, such as the one about the bag of smelly lacrosse clothes. She recognized that Andrew's nervous system had picked up on tension in her tone, and that was what had triggered him into defensiveness.

Grace was able to share her feelings with Andrew and express what was going on inside her with more depth.

"I was feeling so alone and overwhelmed," she told him in one session. "I was raised to be independent, so it's hard for me to ask for help, but sometimes I really need it. When I saw the bag in the closet, all my frustration boiled to the surface, but I didn't know how to make sense of my feelings. I was afraid that if I tried to express myself it would start a fight, so I said nothing. I can see now that my frustration was coming out sideways, and you were picking up on it because I wasn't communicating clearly."

Her accountability made Andrew feel validated, and her vulnerability made him feel closer to her.

In return, he was able to acknowledge how his defensiveness had impacted her.

"I'm trying so hard to make you happy and get it right for you," Andrew shared, "that when I think you're disappointed in me and not seeing my efforts, I'm quick to get defensive. Underneath that I'm feeling hurt and discouraged, but I didn't know how to tell you that. Sometimes I just need to know you see my efforts and appreciate me. Instead of telling you that, I got defensive. I can definitely see how that made it difficult for you to talk to me."

His accountability made Grace feel validated, and hearing his vulnerable feelings made her feel closer to him.

They realized that they simply hadn't known how to identify or express their vulnerable feelings, but now they had a new way of interacting—one that promoted connection, understanding, and secure attachment. This is Self-Connected Communication in action.

Grace stopped avoiding and started to speak up clearly. She chose a different and more team-oriented response, so the entire relationship dynamic changed. As she was less critical, Andrew felt safer and got less defensive. This then made Grace feel safer and encouraged her to be more vulnerable. They stopped getting stuck in bickering loops and pulling away from each other and were able to safely talk about their feelings and needs instead. In doing this, they were leveraging the power of secure attachment to cope, instead of defaulting to avoidance. They ultimately freed themselves from the avoidance trap together.

All couples have to be willing to risk upsetting each other a little bit in the moment, even though it doesn't feel totally comfortable, in order to create the connection that ultimately results from knowing each other more deeply. While Grace and Andrew didn't have the most emotionally secure environment in their childhoods, by acknowledging fears and overriding survival impulses, they were able to overcome avoidance and develop the kind of healthy communication habits that we'll discuss in the next chapter.

Questions for Reflection

- As you thought back on your childhood, what did you notice about your attachment experiences? How did you cope with conflict and distress as a child?
- If you close your eyes and picture your conflict dynamic with your partner as if you were a fly on the wall, what do you notice about your pattern?
- Does your partner protect with defensiveness, dismissiveness, distancing, or fixing from the bad-communication report card? Or do you?
- How do you tend to react to that? Are you aware of what happens that can trigger you into shutting down and avoiding conflict?
- What fears show up for you in a moment of conflict with your partner? Are you aware of the deeper fears that are happening on an attachment level?

PART II

How to Unlock Your Authentic Voice

CHAPTER 3

What Does Healthy Communication Look Like?

"I'm so lucky—my husband and I are not like those couples you see in therapy," Tania says, taking a big sip of her margarita and tossing her hair back off her shoulder.

It's a Saturday and I'm treating her and my other friend Patty to lunch as a thank-you. I had asked them to be my guinea pigs and take my new online quiz on conflict resolution so they could give me some feedback before it went live. We're at a new Tex-Mex place with long-horns on the walls, insanely delicious (and addictive) tortilla chips, and killer fresh guac. Tania and I have already polished off nearly the whole plate as we wait for Patty, who's running late.

"I don't know, Colette," Tania says, with a laden chip paused mid-air. "The questions were all so heavy and serious, and Rick and I are just not like that. We're pretty lighthearted in how we handle things."

I've known Tania for just a few years, having met her through a neighborhood book club, so I don't know much about her dynamic with her husband, Rick. They seem like a great couple, but all I have to go on is what I've seen the few times my husband, Steve, and I socialized with them. Perhaps they really are a securely attached couple, and the security they've developed in their relationship permeates all of their interactions.

These are couples who know a healthy relationship takes hard work . . . but they've done the work, and they've reaped the rewards.

Or Tania could be a "relationship lottery winner"—one of a small number of lucky people who won the relationship jackpot, getting a partner who's easygoing, emotionally intelligent, and willing to over-compensate for the other partner's deficits in ways that serve the overall functionality of the relationship. Despite what couples therapists preach about it taking two, there are those relationships where one person carries more emotional responsibility to make it work. (This can work if the person bearing the emotional labor doesn't find it taxing or feel resentful. For example, in my relationship, I don't mind being the one to initiate most of the communication and repair; it comes very natu-rally to me and I know my partner struggles with it.) Maybe Tania got lucky and married a guy who is happy to do most of the heavy lifting in their relationship. I'm curious to hear more from her, so I nod at her to continue as I scrape the bowl with my last chip.

"What did you find challenging about the quiz?" I asked.

"Well," she said, "it was hard to answer the questions about what I do in conflict because we don't have any."

"Any what?" I said, puzzled.

"Any conflict. We just . . . don't fight," she explained, smiling brightly at first and then wavering as I looked at her, confused.

In an instant I knew that I was likely not listening to a story of secure attachment, and I was definitely not listening to a story of intimacy. As mentioned previously, in a healthy relationship, conflict is accepted as an inevitable, normal aspect of a close partnership. Two people with unique personalities and vastly different backgrounds, often drawn to one another by these differences, are bound to clash. When handled constructively with Self-Connected Communication, however, con-flict can be leveraged as a portal to true emotional intimacy.

The Key to Healthy Conflict:
Self-Connected Communication

A healthy, fulfilling relationship is about depth, meaning, and connection. It's honest and open and real. It's a union between two people who consciously and intentionally continue to choose each other throughout life—who know each other's underlying fears and unhealed wounds and embrace each other in these tender vulnerabilities to become a rock-solid team against the outside world.

It may sound idyllic, but I can tell you it *is* possible to have this relationship—once you have the right tools.

Self-Connected Communication is speaking clearly and directly from your adult self—the part of you that is wise, calm, and grounded. It's a process of going inward to be with and tend to yourself before you approach and interact with your partner. It means being in touch with what you're feeling, thinking, and needing, so you can communicate to your partner with assertiveness, vulnerability, honesty, and kindness. This allows you to feel more confident, empowered, and connected to yourself. It also increases your chances that your partner can hear and respond to your needs; this interaction is a vital part of moving the relationship toward secure attachment.

Through Self-Connected Communication you'll build a new habit of self-expression—a way of being and sharing with your partner that's openhearted and honest. As you embark on this journey, you'll do best if you're willing to practice without expecting perfection. You'll have to give yourself and your partner lots of grace along the way. But the benefits are infinite. It will change the way you live your life and experience your relationship. I see this happen all the time with my clients, but I also speak from personal experience; this is what I've learned to do in my own life. As a result, I'm much happier within myself and my marriage.

The goal is to have a healthy relationship with yourself in which you respond to yourself with love and understanding—a connection to yourself that enables you to reach to your partner with transparency and clarity from a place of self-worth and self-knowing. This creates the opportunity for intimacy, flexibility, choice, learning, and growth. We all have the innate capacity to do this. We merely need to tap into our internal resources and develop the emotional muscle to exercise them. In time and with practice, this process will become more effortless and intuitive.

You've already begun by recognizing the problem: a lack of connection. This chapter begins the process by showing what healthy communication and emotional intimacy actually look like in a real (not idealized) relationship.

What Is Emotional Intimacy?

In a presentation I attended years ago, a brilliant colleague of mine, Reg Morrow, offered a definition that perfectly encapsulates emotional intimacy. She called it "the ability to stay present with your significant other and express your emotions—both pleasant and distressed—and be heard and seen. The same is true for how you receive your partner's varied emotions. Together, you tune in to one another's feelings with empathy."

For me, it means that I let you see my interior world—what I feel, think, and need—and know me as I really am. Because much of my life revolves around food, I like to think of intimacy as the ooey-gooey center of an old-school Duncan Hines brownie, right out of the oven. There's that thin crust that looks like cracked earth and tastes delicious, but there's nothing like biting into the warm center; it's the best part. When you get to that, you're *really* in love with the brownie. When you let your partner into your ooey-gooey center, they get the very best of what there is to know and love about you—your unique self.

True intimacy is letting your partner into your inner world—the good, the bad, and the messy—and trusting them to be a gentle steward of your vulnerabilities. It's an inherently unguarded act, laying down your defenses and risking judgment. It's terrifying to let someone into that warm soft tender place where you are undefended and could be hurt, but without this, the relationship is no deeper than the thin film of sugary crust on the top of the brownie.

When there is genuine intimacy in your relationship, you and your partner share the feelings, attachment fears, and longings we all have, and you're present and responsive to each other. This is **emotional attunement**, which is the heart of intimacy and the biological pathway to how we feel seen, heard, and understood in relationships.

Emotional attunement means being fully present and connected to your partner. When your partner is attuned to you, they look you in the eye, listen to what you have to say, sense and respond to your mood, and are lovingly present and engaged.

As you know from the previous chapter, in childhood we need this type of attunement from our caregivers because we are not yet fully capable of regulating ourselves. Through the loving gaze and attunement of our caregivers, our nervous system regulates, and we feel safe and secure. If we're upset and an adult is attuned to us, we feel that supportive presence, acceptance of our emotions, validation, and empathy. We feel free to experience our emotions and ride the wave of them as they pass through and eventually dissolve. This is the same thing that we need in our adult romantic relationships: comfort, safety, and a sense of being securely attached to our partners in a relationship that offers a safe haven from the world.

Your nervous system is designed to help you feel better when you are connected to your partner during an emotionally painful experience. It's an amazing adaptation. We regulate emotions faster and better with the person we love than we can on our own. When you're attuned and emotionally intimate with someone else, your nervous system is flooded with bonding hormones such as phenylethylamine and oxytocin in a process known as co-regulation. Co-regulation occurs when you and your partner help to steady each other's nervous systems through mechanisms such as close proximity, eye contact, soothing words, and physical affection.

This is why it is normal, and more so optimal, that when you're upset about something, you want to go to your partner to be heard, validated, and soothed. For the same reason, being fixed, dismissed, told to cheer up, or on the receiving end of any of the bad-communication report card responses can be so hurtful.

If you're someone who isn't accustomed to delving into feelings and vulnerability, or haven't had anyone in your life you could safely do that with yet, you might automatically hold yourself back from going there. But it's a risk that comes with tremendous reward. It is through sharing painful feelings that we feel closest to others and create connection. Contrary to what many people believe, sharing painful feelings and vulnerability is what truly connects us. This is how we feel bonded and close to others. Mother Nature has designed us this way because, while suffering is an inevitable part of life, we are not meant to suffer alone. Pain shared feels lighter than pain carried alone.

Healthy couples are masters of co-regulating. They know they can tap into this resource and leverage this superpower for the betterment of their relationship. In essence, attunement and co-regulation create emotional intimacy and enhance secure attachment.

Our primary romantic partnerships provide a unique opportunity to develop ourselves into emotionally mature, securely attached adults. Evolved couples understand that intimacy and maturity are developed in a relationship through having differences and communicating about them. If we don't have someone poking us in those sensitive places, we don't know where we need to grow. This is what allows us to optimize a relationship's deepest potential. Therefore, there is no such thing as "no conflict;" there is only avoidance of conflict . . . and with that comes avoidance of intimacy, however inadvertent it may be.

That's exactly what Tania is really talking about over lunch—pure, simple avoidance, as clean and organic as the now-disappeared guacamole.

She explains that she and Rick don't fight. They don't even bicker. But they also don't really talk about anything of substance. There is a lack of emotional intimacy; they don't open up to each other about their interior worlds, their feelings, fears, or hidden longings. They're genuinely happy and it's not that it's not real; it's just that it's not that deep. They can stay there, floating along at the surface and continue to be okay, as long as nothing happens that rocks the boat.

"I'm probably not very in touch with my emotions, and I like it that way." Tania giggled.

I politely laugh along with her as I'm thinking, *Girl, you're in trouble, and you don't even know it.*

Because in real life, something almost *always* rocks the boat.

It's so tempting to want to live at the smooth surface, where it's light, airy, and easy. Some couples are satisfied with staying active, planning vacations, and having fun with friends. Others are too busy trying to survive to put much energy and attention into developing their relationship. They can run on surface-happy for a long time, oblivious and seemingly content. But when life eventually throws a curveball—a kid with mental health issues, a parent with dementia, a job loss, an infertility struggle, or even an illness or serious accident—then they'll need that deeper intimacy and the skills to sustain it. They simply will not have the depth of maturity to manage a big problem successfully as a team unless they learn those skills in advance. (And believe me, they're *much* harder to develop under duress.)

This reminds me of a couple I once worked with—a cautionary tale for our purposes. Jen and Roman had a full, happy life together for many years. They joked around and didn't see much need to get into feelings. They didn't think they needed communication skills, so they never developed them, and that was okay until multiple disasters hit: His roofing business went under, her father developed dementia, and their oldest daughter began struggling in school. Then they were both drowning, but neither one knew how to ask for support or give it.

Roman didn't feel appreciated and became abrasive. Jen didn't feel comforted and grew cold. They didn't have the infrastructure for communication that they needed, so they stuffed down their grievances and lived in their own separate caves of resentment. Jen's resentment turned to contempt, and then detachment, and by the time she finally spoke up, it was only to ask for a divorce. Roman begged her to go to couples therapy, but by then it was too late. She was too detached for the feelings to return.

Addressing, Sharing, Repairing

Back at the restaurant, my other friend, Patty, finally breezes in, eager to share her experience with the quiz and how she and her husband, Glenn, handle conflict.

"Oh my gosh, I loved it," she gushes about the quiz. "It made me realize how much we're doing right. I think we're good, but sometimes

I wonder. I mean, we're not perfect. The other day I got mad about something, I don't even remember what, and I was like, 'F*** you,' but then I calmed myself down and apologized and we were good. But he can be a dick sometimes, too!"

I laughed. This kind of no-holds-barred commentary is par for the course from Patty. She has always been the kind of friend to tell it like it is. I was encouraged to hear that she and Glenn had a similarly frank communication style at home, too. She continued: "Even if we get heated, we never sweep it under the rug; we always come back to it and say sorry. I feel like I really listen to his feelings, and he listens to mine. We make sure we understand each other, even if we disagree. We're each other's ride-or-die, and I always know that."

"That's beautiful," I say. I'm delighted with her response, and I suspect that my dear friend has the real deal.

Look, maybe her communication style isn't perfect. If Patty were my client, we'd be working to quell the reactivity she exhibits in her arguments with her husband. But there's a lot about what she's describing—including coming back to repair after an "F*** you" slipped out—that sounds like what real, healthy couples do.

Right now, Patty, Tania, and I are having this discussion because of my quiz, but typically women don't talk candidly with one another about the reality of their committed romantic relationships. The ones who do are usually just venting frustrations, and that doesn't help anyone. Most people want to share only the veneer; they're too self-conscious and fearful of judgment to really open up. But by ignoring the real stuff that's going on, we women are often left to struggle alone, not knowing how our relationships compare to the rest. We need to start acknowledging the mess and supporting each other in it—something I hope this important reflective work will help us to normalize!

In relationships of depth, couples relish the complicated mess.

Couples manage conflict constructively because they have habits of communication that sustain them in good times and bad. The building blocks of all constructive conflict are to address, share, and repair.

1. **Address:** They address small issues head on as they arise, knowing that those moments offer the opportunity for connection and intimacy. They don't avoid the little blips, waiting for the tension to pass and never coming back to them, or allow misunderstandings and frustrations to accumulate and turn into resentment.

2. **Share:** They focus on feelings first rather than problem-solving, identifying what they're feeling, sharing those feelings, and asking directly for needs to be met. They co-regulate and attune to each other's emotions, staying present, being responsive, and hearing each other out, leveraging the power of their attachment bond as a source of soothing and comfort.

3. **Repair:** They know that attachment bombs are bound to go off and that perpetual differences will exist, but they apologize often, clear up misunderstandings, and move on. They know that repair isn't about agreeing and solving problems but rather about coming back to reconnect and reestablish emotional safety.

When complaints, feelings, and needs are addressed and expressed, resentments don't accumulate. Every attachment bomb that sets off alarm bells acts as a potential rupture, but also as an opportunity to know each other more deeply and connect through sharing and repairing.

Secure attachment is built in these little moments. Healthy couples harness the power of attachment to create closeness, tapping into how good it feels when you co-regulate with all the soothing and comfort it brings. When you address things that matter and give hurt feelings the proper attention they deserve, those smaller ruptures resolve quickly and easily and you can move on, having preserved the strength and safety of your bond. Both of you feel seen and heard—even if you still disagree and the issue itself hasn't been reconciled.

In a healthy relationship, partners share deeply and repair quickly—strengthening their bond in the process. The more you address, share, and repair, the closer you feel; the closer you feel, the less you fight, and the less there is to address, share, and repair. This is the antithesis of a bickering loop or negative interactional cycle, and instead is a positive feedback loop of connection. Like my friend Patty says of her marriage to Glenn, sometimes they argue and it's not perfect, but they always repair. Because they have the experience of this going well, they are incentivized to continue to address, share, and repair whenever conflict flares. Ultimately, the depth of connection they've fostered leads them to have *fewer* arguments and misunderstandings. And the ones they do have are resolved quickly and without lingering resentment.

Quickly is a key word here. Partners who communicate well don't spend all day having long, drawn-out discussions about feelings. By following these practices, they typically repair quickly and efficiently, so they can get back to living their best lives.

For my husband and me this has become an automatic habit. I own and apologize for my part and express my feelings; he listens and then does the same. And then it's over. This allows us to steer clear of the avoidance trap and also avoid destructive communication, such as circular arguments that go nowhere and leave both of us worn out. Nothing builds up and nothing disconnects. By confronting constructively, couples are free to deal with the issue at hand and move on.

Nonetheless, even healthy couples sometimes get reactive and have a big fight. But because they've developed a habit of being constructive most of the time, they can draw on this to repair without damage. They see each interaction as an opportunity to move the needle toward greater emotional intimacy and a more securely attached relationship.

Here's what I want you to know: You don't have to be perfectly securely attached to have a healthy relationship. You just need to act in ways that foster *more* secure attachment and work to do this in every single interaction.

Creating a relationship of depth means that you address conflict constructively, with healthy behaviors that create more security. No one is perfect or perfectly healed. Everyone is dealing with underlying fears of abandonment and rejection to some degree, and how securely attached a relationship is can ebb and flow over time. That's real life.

The beautiful thing about healthy communication is that it's possible for everyone. You already have everything you need inside you, just like Dorothy in *The Wizard of Oz* with her sparkling red shoes. She had the power all along; she just needed a gentle push to recognize it. Then all she had to do was click her heels to go home—no Oz needed. It's just a matter of tapping into your internal resources, your sparkly red heels, so to speak, to build on your natural capacity for self-expression, attunement, and co-regulation. With a willing spirit and a little effort, you'll make small changes that add up over time, improving the quality of connection you feel and enhancing the security of your bond. Eventually, this new way of communicating becomes a habit until it's second nature to address, share, and repair.

If you're really honest with yourself, there are probably some issues that come up in your relationship that you're not really dealing with because you don't know how to talk about them constructively. Or maybe you're afraid of getting into a dead-end argument. The problem is that this avoidance builds up and leads to the cumulative residue of resentment that can land you in the cave of resentment. You may have a pleasant surface-level relationship for a time, but eventually that may not be enough to sustain you.

It's the messy, human interactions in which you speak up, honor yourself, and tell the truth about what you think and feel that create more secure attachment inside you and between you and your partner. When you know how to self-express effectively, you can address, share, and repair—building intimacy and strengthening your bond.

The Guiding Principles of Self-Connected Communication

One of the first steps to knowing how to speak up effectively is to understand the guiding principles that are foundational to Self-Connected Communication. Keep these core principles in mind as we embark on your journey to finding your voice and then learning to use it in relationship with your partner:

1. **Assertiveness:** Assertiveness means expressing feelings and needs clearly and confidently. It's about unabashedly standing up for what's important to you—and it is not to be confused with forcefulness or aggression. Too often women show up in conflict as meek, self-deprecating, and apologetic. And they're apologizing for . . . what exactly? Simply existing? Bothering someone with their feelings?

   There's no place for that toxic thinking here. Remember that your feelings are always valid. Your experience is your experience. It deserves to be acknowledged by you, for you, and, if you're in a committed relationship, by your partner, too. You have every right to share what you think and feel with your partner in a way that is clear and unapologetic. Clarity is an important, critical component of assertiveness. Mature communication between partners is about identifying what you feel and need and expressing it succinctly, sticking to the one specific issue at hand.

2. **Vulnerability:** I just told you to be assertive, but now I'm telling you to be vulnerable, too. When you don't understand these two concepts fully, they can seem diametrically opposed, and even impossible to reconcile. But in fact, they're excellent bedfellows. Vulnerability is about opening up and going deeper.

Merriam-Webster defines *vulnerable* as "capable of being physically or emotionally wounded" and "open to attack or damage." *Yikes!* No wonder it's so terrifying and counterintuitive. It feels so much safer to protect yourself from potential injury, and when those attachment bombs are going off and your nervous system is screaming *danger*, vulnerability can seem downright insane. But in a relationship, if you show your partner only your protected self, it is impossible to have intimacy and connection. When you're vulnerable, you're letting your partner in. You show your soft underbelly like my dog Vivie, who would roll over the minute I got home, thumping her tail against the hardwood floor, begging me to scratch her pink tummy.

The beautiful thing is that vulnerability invites more vulnerability. When you lead with this, you have a much better chance that your partner will roll over and show you their belly, too.

3. **Honesty:** Your job as a partner is to be honest about what's going on inside you. This is where intimacy comes from. Maybe

that sounds simple, but good-girl conditioning and people-pleasing can make this trickier than it seems. Yet it's the responsibility of every person in a relationship to speak the truth, even when it may be hurtful. Inevitably you may sometimes disappoint or even hurt feelings—but I promise that you can handle that, and so can your partner. Emotional maturity is about being able to tolerate some of this and unhook from your childhood and societal conditioning that has told you it's your job to protect people's feelings at your own expense. It's not. It is your job to tell the truth, the whole truth, and nothing but the truth.

4. **Kindness:** Never underestimate the power of tact. It's how you say it that really matters. Quite simply, being kind is using diplomacy to share your core feelings and needs. You can be assertive and honest while being kind, and in fact this makes all the difference in helping your partner hear you. Kindness doesn't mean supplication; it means thinking about the impact you're having on your partner. This is how you honor yourself by speaking up while also protecting your relationship. You're not sugarcoating; you're saying the truth—nicely.

These guiding principles of Self-Connected Communication allow you to address, share, and repair, while striking the essential balance between preserving the security of the relationship and advocating for yourself.

Our instincts prime us for those fight-or-flight responses that create confusion, fear, and disconnection, so we have to learn how to have a more evolved, mature response to conflict. In our adult romantic partnerships, we must advocate for our own needs and address conflict in ways that preserve the security of our bond and create and maintain emotional safety between us and our partners. When you express yourself according to these guiding principles, you greatly reduce the odds that your partner will receive your message as an attachment bomb, and you increase the chances that what you're trying to say gets through and creates connection.

Sometimes my clients ask me: *What if I'm the only one in my relationship communicating this way?* We'll address how to handle disappointing responses or a lack of communication from your partner in Chapter 9, but the most important thing I really want you to know is that these guiding principles aren't just about taking care of your relationship or getting heard. They're about maintaining a standard of behavior that makes you feel good . . . *regardless* of how your partner responds. It's about having self-respect and honoring yourself. When you rise to the level of communication that you're capable of, you feel confident, bold, and empowered. Not only that—and this is critical— even if your partner can't hear you, as painful as that may be, speaking *your* truth and externalizing what *you've* been grappling with prevents the accumulation of resentment and keeps you out of the avoidance trap.

If you want a healthy, close relationship, you have to do what it takes to get there. Avoidance often feels easier in the moment but takes you further away from the intimacy you crave. Perpetual conflict needn't undermine your bond; it's just a matter of practicing these new behaviors until they become a go-to pattern of communication that enriches your relationship.

Building Secure Attachment, One Interaction at a Time

You met Morgan and Leo in Chapter 1, right after Leo discovered that Morgan had had an affair. Six months into therapy, they've made tremendous progress in healing, rebuilding trust, and working to resolve the avoidant dynamic they'd had prior to the infidelity. They have been learning to address, share, and repair by sending clear signals to each other about what they feel and need in the moment, so they can stay out of the avoidance trap and create a more securely attached relationship.

They're developing intimacy they never had before, because they are addressing each tiny rupture as it arises and implementing Self-Connected Communication to work through conflict in the moment rather than letting it fester. In this way, they've been learning to turn to each other as a resource for comfort, security, and connection, strengthening their attachment every step of the way. They've discovered that they can manage conflict as a team when they lean in differently.

I see them using this new way of communicating consistently in our therapy sessions, and they report that it's happening more and more at home as well. Every time Morgan and Leo address, share, and repair together, they strengthen the neural pathways for this behavior and leave those old fear-based patterns behind. This is due to **neuroplasticity**, the idea that the brain rewires itself as new behaviors are learned and practiced. Because these new choices bring the reward of connection, they're incentivized to replicate them. Success begets success, and through it, they're developing a habit of connection.

The potency of Morgan's affair is slowly receding. Although attachment bombs still go off and Morgan and Leo occasionally get triggered, they're both more confident that they can manage each situation as a team. It's messy but beautiful, and most important, it's working.

Here's how that looks in real time, from a recent session in my office.

"I'm Still Scared That I'll Lose Him"

Morgan and Leo came in joking about how weird it is to look forward to therapy. I noticed how much had shifted in their body language as they sat on the same side of the couch and held hands, looking relaxed.

As they settled in, they began talking about how they're feeling more connected. But even though they've made great strides, those attachment fears are always lurking. It's my job to dig for those places where they might get pulled back into old ways and facilitate Self-Connected Communication. When I probed that day, we uncovered a moment of avoidance that was rife with the potential to set them back but also bursting with the possibility for connection.

Leo set the scene, explaining that he was overwhelmed with stress from his job and needed space to work through it before he talked with Morgan. Later, when he was ready to engage, he noticed that she seemed aloof.

When I checked in with Morgan about this, she said, "I was having a hard day with the kids and feeling stressed out. I kind of wanted to talk to him about my feelings, but he didn't seem open to that at all."

"It sounds like you were needing some emotional support. What did you notice that told you he wasn't available?" I asked.

"I don't know, his body language; he seemed distant. He went into the other room right when he got home and didn't say a word to me. It seemed like he was upset with me."

All of this made sense in the cold, clear light of my office. Leo had been stressed, Morgan had been stressed, and they mistook each other's stress for anger and reacted indignantly in the moment. Anyone who has been in a relationship can relate to this conflict! It could have been resolved right then and there, with a brief healthy exchange in which they addressed, shared, and repaired . . . but Leo and Morgan are still learning. So for now, we're going to do that work together, in our session.

"I'm sure his body language and actions made it harder to approach him," I said, letting Morgan know I understood. "How did you feel inside when you saw those signals from Leo?"

"Confused and alone," she replied. "When he withdrew, I started to feel insecure about the relationship. I wanted to go to him, but I didn't want to get stuck in a loop."

This was Morgan's brain alerting her to danger.

"I can understand that completely," I told her. "This is the man you love more than anyone else in the world, and you nearly lost him. Of course a part of you would be acutely aware of that in the moment and terrified."

I planted the seed for her to bring awareness to her attachment fears, those underlying "blue whales" that were likely present.

"What do you say to yourself in those moments? What's the narrative in your mind about the relationship?" I asked.

"That maybe he's changed his mind and can't forgive me after all." She began to cry. "I'm still scared that I'll lose him."

In that instant when she observed Leo's distance, her mind conjured up the worst-case scenario and told her it was not safe to express her own feelings and needs.

"I told myself I can't go to him with those feelings because it would be selfish. It isn't the right time; he's obviously upset with me. If I bring up my feelings, I'll be making it all about me," she added.

In the moment, this felt like the truth to Morgan. The idea that she should put the needs of others first was something she had been taught throughout her life. This is what good girls do, right? Nobody had ever taught her that she was entitled to make her own needs a priority, even (or maybe especially) when it doesn't feel like the "right time."

Morgan was in her head, talking herself into why avoidance made more sense than sharing from her heart. She had a choice: She could pick avoidance and self-silencing, or she could go for the riskier pathway of vulnerability . . . the one that also offered the possibility of genuine connection to Leo.

The therapy session provided a safe environment where Morgan could practice taking this risk. When attachment fears surface, we can avoid vulnerability, or we can tap into our core capacity to be mature and peaceful and communicate from our most adult part of self. I call this the **Sage Self**. It's essentially our inner Yoda—the part of you that is your most powerful, wise, calm advisor. When you're connected to this part of self, your nervous system is regulated and you're feeling safe. You're able to be present, curious, and engaged, making intentional choices about how you communicate that serve both your well-being and the interests of the relationship. This allows you to become aware of your feelings and needs and advocate for them, just as I was helping Morgan do in session.

When you connect to your calm, wise self, you're creating internal secure attachment and simultaneously establishing the conditions for more secure attachment with your partner. As Morgan was crying and sharing her fears, I helped her connect to her Sage Self, take responsibility for her side of the equation, and communicate effectively. The hope was that this would enable Leo to hear her and respond in kind, with the goal of creating intimacy and connection.

I also helped her tune in to the attachment piece—which is what makes it so scary to communicate; because Leo is so important to her, when he gets distant, she's terrified she could lose him and sometimes too scared to express that.

Speaking the Language of Attachment

It's important to be aware of the attachment forces at play and speak the language of attachment. This means acknowledging the fears that go with the interaction and letting your partner know how important they are to you when you communicate. It's saying things like:

You mean so much to me.
This relationship matters to me.
Because you're so important to me, I get scared to be vulnerable.

Articulating these truths is both disarming and connecting because you're making the importance of the relationship explicit. You always know they're true somewhere in the back of your mind, but you don't always remember to say them out loud. It's tremendously powerful when you do. For your partner it's soothing to hear that they're important to you, and it helps them connect with you from their Sage Self.

I asked Morgan if she was currently feeling some of that fear of vulnerability in her body. When she said she was, I prompted her to turn to Leo and share her fear in the language of attachment—with a simple, clear message from the heart about what was most important.

"When you seem distant, I feel disconnected. Because you're so important to me, I get scared. Then I'm afraid to tell you how I feel because I don't want to push you away more."

Leo responded, "Well, I don't really know what I should do or say when I need to decompress after work. Do I have to just be 'on' the minute I come in because she wants that? Maybe if I take time at the office before I come home . . ." He began to ramble, exiting the moment and galloping ahead to problem-solving mode, thoughts tumbling from his mouth in rapid fire.

It was obvious Leo was in his head, not connecting from his heart.

His response was not unusual. In session, the partner who receives a heartfelt, honest message from the other is often anxious and rushes past a moment that's ripe for connection.

It's not about solving the problem; it's about connecting through feelings. Fixing the surface issue doesn't make a relationship more secure. What does is hearing your partner's vulnerability in the moment and connecting with it viscerally. This is where all the good juju happens—attunement, responsiveness, and co-regulation. When partners vibe in that, they move the needle toward secure attachment. I wanted to help Leo and Morgan get there.

She had just reached for him, letting him into the deeper place where her "blue whale" fears lived. If he raced ahead with word salad on adjacent topics, he would miss her completely and leave her feeling alone in her vulnerability, thinking, *I never want to be that open again.* It wouldn't be because he doesn't care—although that's likely how it would feel to her. Rather, it would be because he was still in a more protective part of himself where his thoughts were running in a million directions. He hadn't yet shifted into his Sage Self, which was exactly what I was about to help him do.

"Leo, Morgan shared her fear that you will give up and leave her, but I notice that a part of you is jumping ahead to problem-solving. I wonder if we could slow down and take in what's happening. Morgan shared that you're so important to her. She is really being vulnerable and reaching for you right now. Can you look her directly in the eye and notice what happens in your body as she shares again?"

He looked skeptical but nodded and turned back toward Morgan, as I prompted her to try again.

"When you came home and went into the other room without speaking to me, I immediately thought you were mad at me. You matter to me more than anyone else, so when I think you're upset with me, I get really scared, and then it's hard to know if it's okay to tell you that."

I validated Morgan and turned to Leo to see how it had landed for him.

"What are you noticing now?"

"It feels different," he said. "I feel a warmth in my chest. I feel safe."

Healthy communication is a full-body experience. It's essential to be aware of what's happening in the nervous system as Leo was in that moment.

He smiled at me and then at Morgan, who reached out to grab his hand again.

Leo felt it in his body because they were co-regulating and really connecting.

Sharing your softer feelings and even being messy and real about them is what brings you closer and makes the relationship into what it's meant to be: a safe container, your most valuable resource in an often cruel, unpredictable world.

When I checked in with Morgan, she, too, was feeling safer and closer.

"It's such a relief to say my feelings out loud," she shared.

Yes, externalizing the feelings lifts the burden. Morgan was building trust within herself and with Leo every time they communicated this way.

This paved the way for Leo to identify and share his feelings, too. He allowed himself to be vulnerable and admit his underlying "blue whale" fear that if he was not perfectly there for her at all times, she might have another affair or leave him. He had denied his own needs and convinced himself to toughen up, pushing everything down to be strong for her. In session, this fear was what had pushed him out of the moment and into his head when Morgan had initially tried to share her feelings. He was able to repair that by apologizing for jumping into problem-solving rather than being tuned in.

This made Morgan feel seen, understood, and open to hearing more from Leo.

Looking her in the eye, he told her, "The other night, I was wanting space, but I didn't know how to tell you, and I was afraid I would upset you. I tried to handle it on my own. It's hard to tell you that I'm scared, but when you open up like you just did, it's easier for me."

Morgan beamed at him and squeezed his hand.

"He never used to open up to me like this; it feels amazing."

"Yeah, I used to think you would see me as weak, but I'm realizing that when we're both vulnerable, we feel the most connected. It's weird that we were both kind of feeling the same way but just didn't know it," Leo added.

Yes! They were both feeling afraid, but when they avoided direct, vulnerable communication, they were alone with those fears. In using Self-Connected Communication they were in it together.

There's truth in the adage that joy shared is twice the joy, and pain shared is half the pain. In turning to each other to address, share, and repair, Morgan and Leo were resourcing their relationship for what it's designed to do: provide comfort and soothe their nervous systems. They were working as a team to manage attachment bombs with clear communication. Both were assertive, vulnerable, honest, and kind, which made it easier for them to hear each other.

Morgan and Leo were able to clear up what was essentially a misunderstanding and dissolve their fears by sharing them, which is true emotional intimacy. What they felt in that interaction in session was the power that came from harnessing attachment in the present moment. And that is what makes their relationship more secure. By coming from their Sage Selves, they created connection and secure attachment right on the spot.

Healthy Communication Looks Like Constructive Conflict

Here's what I want you to take away from Morgan and Leo:

When you're avoiding conflict, you're really avoiding intimacy. Instead you can confront things head on with gentleness and use conflict as a portal to intimacy, depth, and secure attachment. A lot of it is trying and messing up, then repairing when you make a mistake, just like Morgan and Leo. We learn best from failure, not success. Inevitably, even those who've mastered healthy communication still struggle because we're human.

When you confront and communicate the things you're tempted to avoid, you strengthen the security of your bond with your partner and develop more secure attachment with your partner and within yourself. As you learn how to stop avoiding and start connecting more deeply to your own vulnerable needs, you're able to invite your partner into this deeper, more connected place. This is what Self-Connected Communication is all about.

It's a relief when you and your partner verbalize your feelings. It's not just about having knowledge or insight. It's not even about solving a specific issue or problem. It's about sharing the *experience* as it's happening, when you take the risk to offer up your heart on a platter. This is what learning to communicate will bring you: feeling seen, heard, accepted, and connected. When each person takes responsibility to communicate this way, that's when the magic happens.

Remember that your primary task will always be to speak up and honor yourself while preserving the safety and security of the relationship. You don't have to control your partner's response; you merely have to manage your own reactions and come forward clearly. You don't have to fix each other's hurt feelings; you just have to hear and accept them.

Keep in mind that we are not designed to suffer alone; we can turn to our relationship for our attachment needs to be met. A secure relationship is the most valuable resource for comfort, reassurance, and emotional safety.

Questions for Reflection

- Do you and your partner practice these healthy habits of communication? Which do you handle well and which have room for improvement?
- When you need comfort and reassurance, do you tend to go to your partner? If not, what stops you?
- Do you tend to address, share, and repair, working as a team? How does that go for you as a couple?
- Of the guiding principles of Self-Connected Communication (assertiveness, vulnerability, honesty, kindness), which is most challenging for you?
- The Sage Self is who you are at your core; it's the wisest, most loving, mature version of you. Do you have a strong connection to your Sage Self? Do you tend to communicate from this part of you in conflict?

CHAPTER 4

Knowing When You've Been Triggered

"I walked in on him masturbating to porn. He practically threw the phone across the room and then totally lied about it. I feel so betrayed," Gabby said quietly at the beginning of our session.

"I was mortified," Ted muttered, looking down at the ground as if he hoped it would swallow him whole. "It was like being a kid and getting caught by my mom or something. Plus, part of me felt like I was almost cheating on her, and my first impulse was to try to deny it. I don't know what I was thinking."

Before I could respond, Gabby sprang from the couch, her face suddenly flushed bright red, and pointed her finger in Ted's face, yelling, "Are you kidding me? You don't know what you were thinking? I find you jerking off, and you lie to my face? And now you admit you thought it felt like you were cheating and did it anyway? What the fuck? You're disgusting—and a liar and a cheater! I'm done!"

Her whole body was shaking, and her voice had reached an octave that the counselor next door, if not the entire block, could surely hear.

Ted shrank back into the couch, his mouth open in a silent, horrified O. He seemed frozen in shock and at a total loss for what to say.

In a nanosecond they'd both gotten triggered. Gabby had gone from calmly explaining her perspective to screaming at her partner. When Ted said he felt like he was cheating by masturbating to pornography, it set her nervous system on fire.

This reaction didn't surprise me, because triggers exacerbate wounds instantaneously. As their couples therapist for the past six months, I knew there was a history to this issue that predated their relationship, one that still holds power over them to this day.

In fact, Gabby's first husband had struggled with an addiction to pornography, and that addiction had contributed to their divorce. So the mere mention of porn—let alone seeing her new husband looking at it—had been hugely triggering to Gabby. Ted knew about her painful past, and that was part of why he felt so ashamed of his behavior. But Ted had also been triggered by Gabby's reaction—her raised voice, insults, and threats to end the relationship had flooded his nervous system with anger and anxiety.

So when fear hijacked the conversation, they both defaulted to avoidant coping strategies—Ted by shutting down and Gabby by attacking with criticism and blame—that would lead only to further injury and disconnection. They were stuck in a downward spiral of communication . . . unless they made different choices about how to speak to and listen to one another. In our session, it was my job to help them identify their triggers and express themselves clearly.

Everyone has triggers; they are part of the human experience. We're just not always conscious of them. Triggers are your brain's way of keeping you safe by remembering every painful incident from the past and assuming the *worst*, so you'll react protectively and stay alive. Triggers can be a good thing! The catch is that your partner isn't a saber-toothed tiger jumping from the bushes to eat you; they are the person you love pressing on an old wound in real time. This was exactly what was happening to Gabby and Ted in our session, but I felt confident they could repair this rupture if they used their authentic voices and didn't allow triggered reactions to run the show.

In order to unlock your authentic voice, you will first need to be able to recognize when you're triggered in real time so you can be in control of your reactions. Without this self-awareness, you can't possibly engage in meaningful, worthwhile communication, let alone unlearn the avoidant behaviors that aren't serving you and your relationship. This is why owning your triggers is so key in the first phase of Self-Connected Communication—it's a critical part of understanding yourself and how you operate.

Effective communication is a full-body experience. You cannot hear each other or discuss things with your partner—even small things—when your nervous system is dysregulated, which is exactly what happens when you get triggered. Although your partner's behavior triggers you (with something they do or say, or don't do or say), the experience you have as a reaction to it is all your own. It's based on your personal history, your personality, your mood in the moment. By recognizing when you've been triggered, you'll know that something important is happening that needs to be explored—before you self-silence or communicate reactively.

Getting triggered over *small things* is normal in relationships. We're all hypervigilant for threats to our connections. If your partner says or does something really obnoxious that triggers you, you might think, *I don't have time to pause.* But you always have time to take a breath and assess. You just have to get in the habit of noticing and taking charge of your reactions. When you accept that triggers are inevitable in relationships and commit to being more conscious and aware of these moments, you can pause and choose a healthy response.

Your Triggers Have Very Little to Do with Your Partner

Triggers are touchstones to past hurts that reflect what needs to be healed within. They may be activated by something your partner has said or done, or even a stray thought that pops up in your mind out of nowhere. Think of a recent time that you became even mildly upset with your partner, whether it was generated by an internal or external stimulus. What was it that you saw, heard, thought, or experienced that produced a charge of emotion? What were the negative thoughts that crossed your mind or the physical sensations you experienced in your body? If you had been a fly on the wall, how would you have described what you witnessed?

You may be surprised to learn that no matter what triggers you, it is mostly about *you* and has very little to do with your partner. This doesn't mean you don't have a legitimate complaint about your partner! But your experience of the trigger is unique to *you*. It's a product of how you're feeling in that moment (for example, how tired, hungry, or stressed you are), your personality and inborn disposition, how securely attached your relationship is, and your lived experiences. What triggers and bothers one person may be nothing to another. Another woman might have found her partner masturbating to pornography and laughed about it. But when Gabby found Ted doing it, the experience hit on a wound from the past that hadn't fully healed, and the surge of emotion she experienced had understandably overwhelmed her.

Not all triggers are as big or serious as what happened with Gabby and Ted in that session. For example, many clients report getting triggered if their partners play devil's advocate when they're trying to express a simple opinion—always debating the other side of a position. I remember one client telling me that she felt ashamed when her partner did this because the message she got was that she wasn't smart enough. Another woman said that she felt offended when her partner debated her. She took it as a sign of disrespect and an indication that what she had to say didn't matter. On the other hand, a different client reported that when her partner interjects with a counterpoint, she loves it! She finds it stimulating and can't wait to fire back with a fresh argument of her own. Having grown up with parents who were law professors and encouraged lively debates over dinner, she has always welcomed challenging repartee.

In all these cases, the behavior or stimulus was the same (debating), but the reaction inside each woman was unique. The women who were triggered had been invalidated repeatedly in the past for sharing their opinions. They weren't celebrated for having strong ideas and expressing them but rather were met with harsh judgment, were ignored, or were dismissed. This is why they experience painful feelings and interpretations when their partners debate them in the present. On the other hand, the woman who had positive experiences with debates in the past connects that kind of banter with engagement, interest, and a partner who pays close attention to her ideas.

This is why when it comes to identifying your triggers, you must understand that so many different factors—your past experiences, genetic wiring, the health of your relationship, and however hungry, angry, lonely, and tired you happen to be in that moment—will all have a bearing on how you receive and perceive a trigger.

Triggers are like shooting flares, sudden bursts of energy in the body, signaling that something important warrants attention. They provide an opportunity to get clear about your experience and how you're being impacted by your partner. If you follow the thread from the trigger inside, you'll find that it leads you to unhealed hurts and needs. Instead of reacting with avoidant behavior, you need to take a pause to identify the lesson embedded in the trigger and respond with intentionality, which we'll explore in greater detail in the next chapter.

A trigger may be an external stimulus from your partner:

- A tone of voice, such as being brusque, annoyed, or dismissive
- A facial expression, even as little as a raised eyebrow, rolling eyes, or a frown
- The particular words your partner uses, such as something that sounds like an insult or is similar to hurtful comments you received in the past
- A behavior, such as leaving a mess, forgetting to call, or getting defensive

Or a trigger may be an internal stimulus that is self-generated:

- A stray thought that pops into your head
- A feeling that reminds you of something your partner has done
- Fears you have about your partner or your relationship

The goal is to determine what was the stimulus for your internal experience and examine it as objectively as possible, without ascribing meaning. After you've interrupted the trigger, you can pinpoint exactly *what* triggered you and then choose *how* you will respond—either with avoidant behavior (which leads to distance and disconnection) or with Self-Connected Communication (which leads to growth, secure attachment, and a deeper connection with your partner).

Avoidant Behavior versus
Self-Connected Communication

The choice to respond to a trigger with either avoidant behavior or Self-Connected Communication is essentially the choice to weaken or strengthen your attachment bond. To understand the long-term effect of these two responses better, let's examine my clients Oona and Curtis in a triggered moment.

The trigger: Oona is emptying the dishwasher when Curtis comes up behind her, puts his arm around her waist, and gently rubs her hip. Oona is immediately triggered and freezes. She doesn't want Curtis's touch in this moment. To her, it can mean only one thing—he wants sex, and this is his subtle way of signaling his desire. But she isn't at all interested. She's tired, stressed, and worried about her job. Physical intimacy is the last thing on her mind these days.

The Avoidant Reaction

Instead of recognizing that she's triggered and taking the time to process internally and then speak up, Oona retreats in silence. She hopes that if she keeps her distance, Curtis will get the hint. Curtis is hurt and confused by her reaction—he knows she's going through a rough time, and he wants to comfort her. His touch is not meant to signal sex; he just wants to be close to her in this moment. But he doesn't say anything, either. Later that night they go to bed far apart with their backs to each other. Curtis feels rejected. Over time he stops trying to be affectionate.

Initially, Oona is relieved, but later she feels rejected because Curtis never tries to touch her at all anymore. The distance between them grows. Both fear experiencing more rejection and hurting or upsetting the other, so they stifle the discussion. It seems too delicate a topic and neither of them wants to fight, so they don't address it and plunge further and further into disconnection. Years go by, this trend continues, and eventually they divorce.

The Self-Connected Communication Response

But it doesn't have to be this way. If Oona identifies that Curtis's touch was a trigger for her—something that threatened connection in the relationship and elicited an instant reaction inside her—she can respond differently. After she finishes unloading the dishes, she takes some time for herself to get curious about her feelings and what they mean. The story she created is that Curtis only wants sex and doesn't care about how tired and stressed she is. She worries that it isn't safe or possible to be close to him or respond to his physical touch without giving him a green light for sex. She's also irritated with Curtis for touching her—part of her thinks he should just know what she's feeling and leave her alone. *Isn't it obvious that I'm stressed and tired?* she thinks grumpily. In the triggered moment, she's hurt that he's unaware of what she's going through.

Once Oona has taken responsibility for her internal experience and explored it, she's clear about her feelings and needs. She approaches Curtis, asks if it's a good time to talk, and initiates an assertive, vulnerable, honest, and kind discussion.

"When you put your arm around me and rubbed my hip, I felt so anxious that I froze. I thought for sure it meant you wanted to have sex, and that if I welcomed your touch you'd assume I wanted that, too. I *do* want you to touch me, and I want us to be affectionate, but I'm not in the mood for sex right now. Sometimes I'm scared to tell you that because I don't want to disappoint you or hurt your feelings."

Oona holds her breath for a beat, nervous about how this risk to open up will land with Curtis.

But her clear, direct communication helps Curtis understand exactly what's happening rather than having to guess. He's relieved to know that Oona wants to be close to him, because that's all he really wants, too.

"It's totally fine if you're not in the mood right now," he said. "I wasn't even thinking about sex, actually—although you're right that often that's what's on my mind. I'm happy if we can just be affectionate. And I really appreciate you telling me how you felt. When you pulled away from me, I was triggered by your reaction and I felt rejected. I should have noticed this and told you about it. I will make the effort to do that next time."

Oona's vulnerability invites Curtis's vulnerability. They vow to keep the lines of communication open about their sex life and what's going on inside them emotionally. They go to bed that night spooning, contented, and connected. This trend continues and their marriage lasts.

If you let yourself get hijacked by your triggers, it's unlikely that your partner will stay engaged and respond to you with the softness and understanding that you deserve. Self-Connected Communication invites a more vulnerable response from your partner and opens a pathway to the possibility of deeper connection, intimacy, and secure attachment.

The hope is that if you recognize your triggers in the moment and initiate Self-Connected Communication, your partner will join you in this work as Curtis did with Oona. Unfortunately, it's also possible that your partner won't reciprocate your vulnerability. You have no control over how your partner responds. But you can do your part to create the most favorable conditions possible for deeper understanding and connection. Although it would be disappointing if your partner can't or won't meet you in that vulnerable place, remember, either way, you're engaging in Self-Connected Communication for *you*. Your voice and your experience deserve to be heard, and it's always worth taking the risk.

How to Identify a Trigger

Body sensations are often the first clue that you've been triggered. There is that critical moment when an attachment bomb goes off and suddenly everything has shifted. There's a charge—you can feel your frustration or irritation. Beneath that, in your body there is fear—of getting into a fight, of having an interaction that brings pain or imperils your relationship. A protective part of you wants to react right off the cuff or just stuff the feelings down and swallow your words.

The first step to properly identify your trigger is to redirect your energy from focusing on your partner to getting curious about yourself. It's about scanning your body and recognizing that something is happening within. There's more to this moment than you think, and now's the time to do that important detective work to better serve yourself and your partner! To start, get in the habit of saying to yourself, *Let me take a moment to understand what's really going on here.*

To assess what's going on when you feel yourself being triggered, ask yourself:

- *Can I be curious right now?*
- *Is my nervous system regulated?*
- *Am I speaking to share or to control?*
- *Am I operating from fear or love?*

Sometimes when you feel yourself being triggered, you may just need to slow down for a moment and take a breath or two to recalibrate, and then you can proceed. With awareness, you can assess how capable you are of speaking constructively. If you're calm, curious, and clear, then you know you can speak up. If not, you need more time to process your experience and regulate yourself, which means you need to a take a pause (a concept we'll dive into more in the next chapter). You're building a muscle for intentional and conscious communication. If you can't access your Sage Self—the wise, regulated, adult part of you—then you're not in the position to communicate with your partner.

TEN BREATHS TO CONNECTION

The following exercise can help you interrupt your reaction to a trigger so you can process your experience.

Once you notice that you're triggered, pause and take ten slow deep breaths.

Close your eyes and count the breaths as you go, following each breath in through the nose all the way down into your abdomen for a count of four. Notice your lungs filling up and then releasing all the air out through your mouth for a count of eight.

Continue to inhale for a count of four and exhale for a count of eight.

Don't judge yourself if you get distracted; it's perfectly normal. Simply bring yourself back to the breath and resume counting.

When you're finished, notice how you feel. Were you able to focus through all ten breaths? Do you feel a little more connected and grounded inside?

This exercise helps you get present, become more consciously aware, and interrupt whatever is happening externally in the moment. It regulates your nervous system and sets the stage for turning inward to explore your thoughts and feelings. With practice you will get better at noticing that you're triggered as it's happening, rather than afterward.

The health of your relationship depends on making a commitment to self-awareness. As you do, you'll get better at intuitively listening for clues inside and instinctively connecting with yourself. Your observing ego, which is your ability to witness your experience as it's happening, will become stronger, and you'll know how to notice and evaluate the present moment to make decisions that serve both your well-being and the good of the relationship.

In the moment, awareness is essential so that you can pause and process your experience before you react. To do this you have to interrupt the trigger and identify it rather than letting it hijack you. You don't operate off the cuff from a place of fight or flight and survival, and you don't bite your tongue and stuff your feelings, either, self-abandoning to keep the peace. Rather, you pause and get curious about your internal experience and then choose your response.

Remember that in conflict, you can get triggered easily because your partner is so important to you. In a way, this is good thing! It means your internal radar is ultra-sensitive to potential threats to your relationship. But these deeper "blue whale" fears of rejection, abandonment, and loss of connection you learned about in Chapter 2 are easily activated and often unconscious. If you're not paying attention, you can get hijacked by these protective parts of yourself that want to yell, run away, or criticize—all avoidant behaviors that lead to more disconnection. You won't be able to accurately process your experience or communicate effectively about it. This is why it's essential to interrupt a trigger.

Reacting versus Responding to a Trigger

Reacting to a trigger is when you behave protectively out of impulse. It's any behavior that avoids real, vulnerable self-disclosure. For example, reacting is when you snap at your partner, yell, name-call, withdraw, or stonewall in the face of a trigger. It's also when your partner reacts with those frustrating bad-communication behaviors—defensiveness, dismissiveness, distancing, and fixing. These are all protective and avoidant reactions to a perceived threat.

On the other hand, **responding** is thoughtful adult communication from your Sage Self. It's choosing to address and share from the most adult part of yourself so you can repair. This means telling your partner about what you experienced inside when you were triggered in a clear, respectful manner. Any time something hurtful happens, you should be addressing it by responding rather than reacting. Your ultimate task is to express your feelings from a self-focused place and share the impact of a trigger, rather than pointing out what your partner's doing wrong.

An example of a reaction would be if you said something like "You're so rude; why do you talk to me like that?" in an elevated tone of voice. Conversely, a response would sound something like "When you speak to me this way, I feel hurt and offended," in a calm, even tone. The difference between reaction and response is that the latter focuses on *you* and is delivered when you're regulated. Then you can clearly share what's happening inside without blaming your partner. This gives them the best chance possible of being able to hear you and respond well in kind.

Remember, the problem isn't that you and your partner get triggered; triggers are inevitable in a close committed relationship. The problem is how you react to these triggers. If you behave protectively from parts of you that are survival-based and ready to guard you from potential danger, you'll likely trigger your partner in return.

When you react with protection, you may trigger your partner into operating out of their own self-protection. Then you're stuck in a fight-or-flight feedback loop of reactions and counterreactions where neither of you is heard or understood, and feelings and needs go untended. It becomes a self-fulfilling prophecy, as the fears that drove you to protect yourself in the first place wind up feeling true and you're further disconnected from your partner.

On the other hand, when you notice your trigger and take a pause, you tune in, manage your response, and communicate from your Sage Self when you're emotionally regulated.

There is a difference between destructive and constructive conflict. When conflict comes from fear, it can lead to chaos and wounding. Fear will always lurk beneath the surface because the relationship is so important to you. But you don't have to let fear run the show. You can be with the part of you that holds the fear inside and come to the present to realize you're safe now.

When communication is constructive and intentional, it leads to growth, connection, and secure attachment. When you come from love, there is curiosity, understanding, and acceptance. You're able to listen to yourself and your partner. You'll know you're ready to communicate when you feel this calm, regulated state in your body. This is why connecting to yourself is so crucial.

Gabby and Ted Respond Instead of Reacting

Once I helped Gabby and Ted de-escalate from their flare-up in session, they were able to identify their triggered states and, with my guidance, communicate by responding to each other instead of reacting with avoidant coping strategies.

"I was enraged when I heard you say you felt like you were cheating and did it anyway," Gabby said. "Not only was I angry that you lied to me, but it also took me right back to those times with my ex-husband when his pornography use consumed our relationship, and he was dishonest about it all the time. I'm sorry for threatening the relationship, I don't want to end things with you, but underneath my anger I do feel sad, hurt, and afraid I can't trust you. I need to know that you get how serious this is for me and that you're going to work to rebuild my trust so I can feel safe again," Gabby continued tearfully.

"I do get it, and I'm so sorry for betraying you," Ted said. "I got triggered when I heard you say I was disgusting and you were done, because I thought you were gonna leave me. I was so overwhelmed and scared in that moment that I didn't know what to say. But I understand why you feel the way you do, and I take full responsibility for what I did. I should have discussed using porn with you in advance to make sure you were comfortable with it, especially knowing what happened with your ex. And I definitely shouldn't have lied to you about it. I understand why you feel betrayed, and I am willing to do whatever it takes to rebuild trust."

Gabby and Ted moved to the center of the couch and hugged, crying softly together. There was still a lot of work to be done, but they were in it together now—connected to their Sage Selves, communicating like mature adults, and moving toward healing as a team.

Taking a Couples Time-Out

We don't typically have a couples therapist on call at home to facilitate repair as I'd done in session with Gabby and Ted! So we have to referee ourselves when we get triggered. The good news is that everyone is capable of doing this, with self-awareness and a solid plan.

If you're triggered when you're in the midst of interacting with your partner, it's best to take a time-out. This isn't a concept unique to my work with clients—most couples therapists advocate for some kind of break in communication to prevent reactivity. The advice is to cease all communication and remove yourselves from your shared space, so both of you can regulate and process your internal experience (which we'll discuss in depth in the next chapter) before you communicate. This works best when partners agree in advance to using this relationship tool, make a specific plan for how they'll do it, and commit to implementing that plan when triggers arise.

The Benefits of a Couples Time-Out

The purpose of the time-out is to protect the relationship. It's not true that you have to resolve things before you call it a night. "Don't ever go to bed angry" is a myth. That isn't always realistic for our nervous systems or best for the relationship. If one or both of you are triggered, it's much better for your relationship to pause and come back to your discussion when the time is right. Often going to bed *without* resolution is the healthiest choice you can make. But if you do that, it's essential that you both commit to coming back to the table soon—and that you honor that commitment. If you take a time-out, you must return at the designated time. This certainty creates emotional safety.

For the person who is more anxiously attached, not resolving things immediately can feel very stressful. If this is you, you'll need to self-soothe and remind yourself that this is simply about protecting your relationship from reactivity. Take comfort in knowing that you'll reconnect at the designated time, and the relationship is okay.

On the other hand, the person who is more avoidantly attached experiences the separation of a time-out as a relief rather than a strain. If your partner is like this, don't interpret it as a sign that they don't care about the relationship. It's about how they naturally prefer to regulate themselves. If you're more avoidantly attached, you'll need to self-soothe and remind yourself of the importance of returning to your partner to create safety as soon as possible.

Some people seek comfort in resolving and feel stressed until that happens, while others seek comfort in going off by themselves to process internally until things feel calm enough to reengage. The time-out makes it possible to meet in the middle. You know what to expect— that you won't avoid or argue destructively, and that you'll resolve things when conditions are ideal.

A time-out protects your relationship and prioritizes it, even (or especially) when you're triggered. It will keep you from engaging in counterproductive behavior—lashing out, shutting down, or withholding—that's all too common when we're reacting in the moment. Those reactions are natural, but they send scrambled signals to your partner. Problems get bigger instead of cleared up.

The relationship time-out prevents escalation. In my clinical experience, when partners agree to a time-out policy and honor it, it works wonders. On a personal note, my husband and I have our own time-out plan that we use and find extremely effective in preventing unnecessary and harmful escalations. Ours works like this: If either one of us feels triggered and we're not ready or able to communicate clearly and kindly in the moment, we take a time-out. One of us says, "Time-out," and we immediately stop talking and go into separate rooms to cool down and process our own internal experiences. We wait forty-five minutes (my husband needs a longer cooldown period than I do!) and then return to check in. At that time we either decide to take more time, if needed, or to repair and hear each other out with curiosity, respect, and understanding.

A couples time-out works for us, and it works for many of the clients I see as well.

Lisa and Marni's Time-Out

My clients Lisa and Marni learned to use the same time-out strategy whenever one or both of them were triggered, and they found it deeply beneficial to nurturing their connection. They have been together for eleven years, and they're still very much in love and committed to their partnership. However, before they learned Self-Connected Communication, they tended to avoid conflict when they got triggered by suppressing their feelings, venting tension through passive-aggressive digs, or getting into bickering loops over mundane issues that concealed deeper attachment fears and longings.

One pain point in their relationship was that Lisa longed for more quality time and affection than she was currently getting from Marni. On the flip side, Marni was in an extremely busy season of life. She was working full-time and had recently started a graduate program in human resources. Her longing was for Lisa to understand that she didn't have a lot of emotional energy for the relationship right then and to give her some grace.

After a lot of frustrating conflicts that went nowhere, they made a plan in advance to implement a time-out whenever either of them was triggered or derailed. They agreed to say, "Time-out," and use the capital *T* hand signal. They committed to honoring the time-out once either one of them called it, and to returning after a thirty-minute break to check if both were regulated enough to communicate effectively.

One evening, Marni came home from work late and joined Lisa in the family room to watch TV, taking a seat on the other side of the couch rather than next to her.

Lisa was immediately triggered by Marni choosing to be far away from her. She reacted instead of responding. "Are you gonna sit all the way over there?" she asked with a discernible edge in her voice.

Unsurprisingly, Marni was triggered by Lisa's reaction, which she experienced as a passive-aggressive accusation. Marni reacted instead of intentionally responding from her Sage Self. She rolled her eyes, threw up her hands, and huffed, "Seriously? Can you just give me a freaking break for once?"

Lisa could feel her body flooding with adrenaline but was self-aware enough to observe this reaction. In this triggered moment her instinct was to fire back, but remembering their plan, she called a time-out using the *T* hand signal and saying, "Time-out." Lisa immediately went into the bedroom, set a timer for thirty minutes, and began counting her breaths to get regulated. During that time-out, she realized that underneath the trigger, she had been feeling hurt and lonely in Marni's absence. She craved more affection to reassure herself she was still a priority.

Simultaneously, Marni used the time-out to process her own triggered experience. She realized that she was feeling angry and overwhelmed, and deep down she was lonely, too. She craved more flexibility and understanding from her partner.

When the thirty minutes were up, Lisa returned to Marni. Since both felt regulated and had access to their Sage Selves, they were able to apologize and express their feelings and needs clearly. They had a healthy discussion that allowed them to be responsive to each other's needs. Lisa promised to be more flexible and understanding of Marni's schedule, and Marni agreed to come home earlier at least one night a week and make sure they shared more physical affection. They both left the interaction feeling more connected and clear about the changes they would make to meet each other's needs. They also prevented the accumulation of resentment, which would only keep them prisoners of the avoidance trap.

Building Your Own Couples Time-Out

You may want to approach your partner and invite them to develop a couples time-out plan with you. I like the version of a couples time-out from Dr. Susan Campbell and Dr. John Grey's book *Five-Minute*

Relationship Repair and have given an adapted, CliffNotes version here. How to plan and execute a couples time-out:

1. Agree on a signal or word that indicates the need for a time-out.
2. Decide how long the time-out will be (twenty minutes at minimum and up to twenty-four hours depending on your individual needs).
3. When needed, use your signal or word to call a time-out.
4. Remove yourself from the space (obviously that won't work if you're triggered in a moving vehicle, so in that case, just be silent).
5. Take the agreed-upon amount of time to regulate and process.
6. Return to your partner at the designated time to check in.
7. Ask if they are regulated enough to communicate.
8. If both of you are regulated, proceed; if either or both are not, take another time-out or agree to revisit the topic at a later time.

This time-out plan will allow you to get regulated enough to repair. Dr. John Gottman's research tells us that the ability to repair is what makes or breaks couples, and the sooner the better. However, everyone's nervous system is different, and some come back to baseline more quickly than others. Physiologically it's not really possible to come back to your Sage Self in fewer than twenty minutes, so keep that in mind. Know yourself and honor what works for you. If you need three hours to calm down, then take them. What's important is to know your nervous system and be realistic about it. It's equally important to come back to your partner and address the issue once you've reached a regulated state.

We'll explore how to have these repair conversations in greater depth in Part III. For now the important thing is to have thought through your own needs around taking a time-out, so you can protect your relationship from avoidant behaviors.

This prevents you from getting stuck in the avoidance trap and allows you to disclose the deeper layer of vulnerability that creates connection. When you show up differently, you're more likely to get healthy clear communication from your partner.

The time-out and subsequent pause also allow you to be there for your most important relationship—the one you have with yourself. In the next chapter we'll dive into what to do during the pause so you learn how to identify what you feel and need, regulate yourself, and use your voice to speak up effectively.

Questions for Reflection

- Are you aware of your most common triggers?
- How do you behave when you're triggered? Do you typically react or respond?
- Is it difficult for you to regulate your nervous system in triggered moments?
- How long does it typically take you to calm down once you've been triggered?
- Have you ever tried to take a time-out when you get triggered during relationship conflict?
- If so, was it successful? If not, where did you get stuck?

CHAPTER 5

Pausing to Process Your Thoughts and Emotions

Veronica and Paul came to therapy after thirty years of marriage because they don't agree on whether they should sell their house and move—and they don't know how to talk about it. They're in their sixties, and Paul is about to retire from his corporate job. Veronica worked as an accountant in her early years but eventually stayed home with the kids. They made that decision together and neither has regretted it. Now that their children are grown and with kids of their own, Paul wants them to sell their home and move to the beach on the other side of the state. For years he has dreamed of the sounds of the surf, daily walks on the sand, and pocketing the money they'd make off their five-bedroom house.

Veronica is irritated every time Paul hints at moving to the beach. She wouldn't mind getting a small vacation place and being there from time to time, but the thought of selling the house in which they raised their family and resided for nearly three decades is a hard no. She has for years quietly refused to have any discussion about moving to the beach full-time. In fact whenever Paul expressed an interest in going over to look at condos, she changed the subject. She didn't want to get into it. Paul doesn't want to argue, either, and hopes eventually she'll magically change her mind.

A decision needs to be made, but their different desires feel threatening and unresolvable, so they avoid the conversation entirely. Neither one of them knows how to bring up a difficult topic to address, share, and repair. They've never learned how to process and share their thoughts and emotions, so they have little understanding of their own needs—much less each other's. They fill this void of understanding with **Negative Partner Stories** they've created about the other's position (*she's being stubborn; he's being selfish*).

They're at a stalemate, and it remains to be seen how or if the question of moving can be resolved to their mutual satisfaction. But they have a bigger problem, which is that their avoidance is creating distance, distrust, and animosity. Because they haven't developed the skills to share their thoughts and feelings, the issue about moving has driven a wedge between them. It has gotten much bigger than it would have been if they had been practicing Self-Connected Communication.

In their first session, Veronica explained that Paul had announced a surprise vacation at a very nice resort on the same beach where he was hoping to move. Veronica was sure she knew exactly what that meant. He was trying to manipulate her into doing what she didn't want to do—move. This wasn't the first time something like this had happened.

Years before, Paul had uprooted her from a neighborhood she really loved to their current home. Veronica had gone along with Paul's decision back then, but she resented him for it. That move had been prompted by an emotional affair Veronica had with a male neighbor, back when Paul had been working around the clock and she had felt neglected. Although it had never become physical, Veronica and the other man had taken walks together, expressed feelings for each other, and written each other notes. After Paul found one of their notes, there had been a huge blowup—but the underlying relationship issues were never resolved. Paul had simply moved them to a new location. Although Veronica understood why he'd reacted that way and realized that her secret relationship had been wrong, she'd resented the move and thought it unnecessary.

Now, when Veronica heard that Paul had planned a vacation to the beach, she was convinced that he was once again trying to manipulate her into moving. She was sure he hadn't ever forgiven her for her long-ago transgression and was going to find a way to force her to move once again. In her mind it was always all about him. Her Negative Partner Story was that Paul didn't care about her feelings and would make sure he got what he wanted.

As Veronica mentioned in our session, her feelings about moving were similar to those she had experienced as a child, when she was forced to move nine times because of her mother's fleeting romantic relationships.

As for Paul, he was convinced that Veronica had never really cared about what was important to him. After all, she wouldn't even *consider* moving, much less talk about it. He'd always felt not good enough for her, which was dramatically confirmed years ago by her emotional affair with their neighbor. And when Veronica recently mentioned how several of her friends were getting divorced and seemed happy about it, his Negative Partner Story was reinforced. He suspected that now that their kids were out of the house, Veronica also wanted a divorce, and that deep down, *this* was the real reason she didn't want to move to the beach.

Paul also revealed that when he was twelve years old his parents had pulled the rug out from under him when they announced they were getting a divorce. He hadn't seen it coming then, and perhaps the same thing was happening now.

"I don't want to leave our home or live so far away from my friends," Veronica shared.

"No, it's because you've always resented me," Paul responded, "and this is how you're finally showing it."

Veronica threw up her hands and turned to me. "See, there's no point trying to talk about it. I either have to do what he wants or I get this."

When Paul told Veronica that the trip he'd planned was an earnest attempt to spend time with her at his favorite beach spot, she didn't believe him.

"You're just saying that to look like the good guy in therapy, but I know that trip is really about trying to force me to move to the beach."

A common scenario was playing out: Partners make assumptions about each other's thoughts, intentions, and motivations, and don't believe each other, even when the truth is shared. They assume the worst without leaving space for the possibility that their assumptions are wrong.

How did Paul and Veronica get here?

They had never talked about or repaired the attachment injuries that occurred in their marriage years earlier: for Paul when Veronica had an emotional affair; and for Veronica, when Paul made them move in the aftermath. Stuck in the avoidance trap, they had also failed to communicate openly and vulnerably about both the big and little things that bothered them throughout their marriage. They suppressed their feelings and clung to their Negative Partner Stories as incontrovertible truths instead of sharing them as tentative hypotheses.

When it comes to our romantic partnerships, there is no concrete truth but rather two subjective realities living side by side. We must pause to process our emotions and thoughts so we can identify what we need and share it with our partners, instead of avoiding the discussion and doubling down on false narratives and righteous indignation.

When you pause to process your thoughts and emotions—and share them with assertiveness, vulnerability, honesty, and kindness—you open the door for understanding and connection.

The Power of the Pause

Many couples I work with say, "I don't like conflict," and I get it. Who does? It's scary and uncomfortable when something is fraught with the potential to disconnect you from your partner and cause pain. Yet when conflict is managed well, it offers the greatest potential for connection, closeness, and growth. The pause is a little bubble of time that allows you to process your emotions and thoughts, identify your needs, and self-soothe. When you have time to regulate and reflect, it's much easier to communicate effectively.

There are two scenarios in which you might use the pause. One is when you're triggered, as you learned in the previous chapter. The other is when you have an important issue to address—such as a particular complaint about your partner, or a difference in parenting, spending habits, or desire to relocate like Veronica and Paul—anything that has been weighing on your mind that you're nervous to bring up.

During the pause you'll be connecting to yourself to do quite a bit of internal work before you actually speak up. Connecting to yourself is different from figuring things out rationally, which rarely works when emotions are involved. Self-Connected Communication means connecting to the full kaleidoscope of your experience—including thoughts, feelings, and sensations—and allowing them to unfold as intended. This inner work will support and bolster you, regardless of how your partner responds. So without further ado, let's dive into the three steps one must take to properly pause, which we will explore at length in this chapter:

1. Tune in to your emotions.
2. Challenge your Negative Partner Story.
3. Tend to your inner child.

The pause enables you to break the cycle of avoidance by taking control of your reactions and speaking up from your Sage Self—the wise, gentle steward of your needs. This may be the most important piece of Self-Connected Communication. It's a total game changer once you learn to pause and process, rather than react with avoidant behaviors. Had Veronica paused to process the first time she was bothered by the thought of moving, she might have gotten a sense of connection and understanding from Paul rather than the dismissal she received in my office.

There is no guarantee Paul would have responded well had Veronica practiced Self-Connected Communication, but she would have felt better regardless from pausing to take care of herself emotionally and express herself clearly. Many of us believe (whether consciously or unconsciously) that our partner is the only possible source of validation that means anything. If they notice us/approve of us/endorse us, we must be doing okay . . . or at least, so our (subliminal) mind says. But it's simply not realistic to expect that your partner will be able to perfectly provide this kind of support at all times, no matter how well you communicate.

You can, however, always give *yourself* validation.

Let me repeat that: You can give *yourself* validation, and there's no barrier when the validation comes from within.

This is where the pause comes in—it gives you the space to tend to your feelings and needs with the validation and compassion you deserve. When you take a pause to give yourself time and space, you're telling yourself, "My needs matter. They warrant consideration. They deserve to be spoken." You gain a sense of peace and clarity no one can take away from you.

Tune In to Your Emotions

Sometimes it's hard to identify feelings, much less share them with your partner. But accurately naming your feelings is an essential part of organizing your experience and regulating your nervous system. It's a way of making sense of what's happening inside and building a bridge to closer connection with your partner. When you're in conflict with your partner, you may be aware of surface emotions like frustration, irritation, annoyance, or even anger. But if you dig deeper, there are usually underlying primary emotions such as hurt, sadness, fear, loneliness, and shame that provide critical information. They are signals in your body that point you to your attachment needs. You have to notice what you feel in order to know what you need.

Embracing your emotions and listening to the messages they tell you may feel overwhelming. So let me break it down for you—try this six-step process for tuning in to emotions when you're taking a pause:

1. ***Notice your body sensations.*** You may notice a heaviness or tightness in your chest, a pit in your stomach, tingling in your limbs, an accelerated heart rate, or tension in your jaw. Many of us skip right over these physical sensations. Rather than doing that, take a moment to tune in to them.

2. *Name the corresponding emotions.* Once you notice what's happening in your body, start to map that to an emotion or emotions that you may also be feeling. These body sensations correspond to emotions such as frustration, irritation, annoyance, anger, resentment, and anxiety. Take a moment to name those sensations and emotions.

3. *Get curious.* Allow your emotions to flow and bring the curiosity of your Sage Self to witness. Ask yourself, *What is this feeling telling me right now? Is my tight stomach a sign of nervousness? Is tension in my jaw a sign of anger?* By asking yourself directly you'll be much more likely to get an answer about what you're feeling and why it matters.

4. *Take your time.* Don't rush this process. Snap judgments are not your friend. Take the time you need to explore your feelings more deeply. Do you feel alone, afraid, hurt, abandoned, rejected, sad, or ashamed beneath your surface-level anger? It's important to sit with your superficial feelings long enough to allow your deeper, truer feelings to make themselves known.

5. *Offer yourself validation.* Put your hand on your heart and tell yourself your feelings make perfect sense. Thank your emotions for showing up to guide you.

6. *Give yourself compassion, love, and acceptance.* Talk to yourself with the compassion you would extend to your best friend or closest loved one. If someone you cared about was upset, you wouldn't tell them that they were being ridiculous and they should get over it already or that they were being silly, so don't do that to yourself. Speaking compassionately to yourself when painful

emotions arise is one of the most powerful ways to regulate your nervous system.

Let's practice so you get more familiar with the process:

TUNING IN TO AND EXPLORING EMOTIONS

Set a timer for five minutes. Close your eyes and turn your attention inward. As you tune in, see if you notice any sensations. Are you feeling any emotion right now? Scan your body through the following steps, and allow whatever is happening to come forward:

Take a couple of deep breaths, and start at the top of your head. Moving slowly downward, scan each part of your body, from the top of your head to your face, neck, chest, back, stomach, hips, genitals, legs, all the way down to your feet, just noticing anything you become aware of.

If you get distracted, notice this without judgment and gently bring your attention back to your body. There is no need to force anything to happen or put pressure on yourself; you're simply becoming aware of whatever is there that might remain outside your conscious awareness.

What did you notice? Maybe there is a little energy in your chest or limbs or maybe some tension in your jaw. See if you can simply make note and hold some curiosity for what that sensation may have to tell you about your feelings.

Get curious. What emotions can you name? What does that feeling or part of you want you to know? Are any deeper feelings present below the surface? Acknowledge and allow any and all feelings you have. Stay present with them as you offer yourself validation and compassion; then return to the room.

When you're feeling something, a part of you is trying to get your attention and deliver an important message. With awareness, you can tune in and respond with curiosity, love, and care. Your emotions will communicate what's necessary and then dissolve naturally. What fuels and intensifies emotions most is trying to disown them or push them away. On the other hand, when you acknowledge and allow your feelings, your pain eventually subsides. By leaning in to your feelings from your Sage Self, you gain awareness and insight about what you need and feel more grounded.

Challenge Your Negative Partner Story

Have you ever had an ugly thought about your partner in the heat of the moment? Even if you're in the most loving relationship, you probably have! When your partner does that thing that drives you nuts, your brain makes a snap judgment about safety or danger and then creates meaning, often a false narrative of what really occurred. A part of you may see your partner in an unflattering light in that reactive moment, but it doesn't necessarily reflect your global perspective on the relationship. Fifteen minutes later you may not even remember what triggered you or the Negative Partner Story it generated.

This is why it's essential to take a pause in such a moment—not only to process your feelings but also to notice thoughts without attaching too much meaning to them.

The brain is a meaning-making machine, and unfortunately it tends to run negative. This is simply something that we do—create stories to make sense of everything that happens in our world. In her book *Rising Strong*, Brené Brown popularized the phrase "The story I tell myself . . ."

to refer to those narratives we create to make meaning of what our partners are doing and why they're doing it.

But you can't believe everything you think, especially during conflict. No matter how well you know your partner, your narrative of their motives is often wrong. As you've learned, the reptilian survival brain makes snap appraisals about safety and danger based on what it first detects, often leading to automatic and flawed meaning-making. If unchecked and unrepaired, these stories can do a lot of damage. You can easily build a case against your partner in your head that comes to feel like the absolute truth and begins to steer the trajectory of the relationship off the rails.

The truth is that what goes on in your mind can make you far more miserable than your partner can.

Your thoughts can turn really negative in triggered moments. Many committed partners have told me about thoughts of divorce, moments of hating their partner and even wishing their partner would die. On the less intense side, you may have thoughts about your partner being insensitive, unfair, and unreasonable. Sometimes your inner narrative about your partner is telling you, _See, they're a jerk and it's all their fault._ It feels _so_ much better to blame in the moment, even though blaming does nothing but give your power away.

In my own marriage, I notice that my Negative Partner Story often follows a familiar track. If my husband does or says something that makes me really angry, my thoughts can go to the extreme very quickly with feelings of blame, panic, hopelessness, and a predictable urge to flee. This stems from my hyper-independence and need for self-reliance when my parents were separated and fighting a lot during my childhood. Now in the heat of a triggered moment with my husband, I might think something like _I have to get out of here. It's never going to_ *change. He will never really get me. I should have known better than to think I could really count on him or anyone else. It's much safer and better to run and be on my own.*

In a moment of conflict, you may also have negative thoughts about yourself—about being unloved or unlovable, not being good enough, being unfairly mistreated or perpetually misunderstood. Sometimes these thoughts show up as absolutes—*They always forget; they never listen; they don't care.*

These negative and distorted thoughts are in part fueled in the moment by the attachment threat. Powerful fight-or-flight emotions, such as anger and fear, create distorted thoughts. As you've learned, you also filter everything you hear and experience through the lens of your unique personality, cultural milieu, past painful experiences, and unhealed hurts. Additionally, the overall health and security of the relationship will influence the meaning you make of even the smallest interaction with your partner. Even stress, hunger, and exhaustion can contribute to the story you tell yourself.

When you're triggered or ruminating about an issue that feels like a threat to your connection, it's often the meaning you make of what happened that creates the biggest problem. It's normal for this to happen, but if you habitually subscribe to your first negative interpretation, it can become dangerous to your relationship over the long term.

In order to properly pause and bypass avoidant coping strategies, you'll need to accept that your narrative of what's happening is likely *not* what's happening. It may feel true in the moment, but it's distorted. By pausing to notice your thoughts and engaging your Sage Self to challenge them, you can regulate your nervous system and prevent these distortions from hijacking the relationship. Simply notice them, let them settle, and challenge them. The goal is to become more conscious of your inner narrative and hold it lightly. You can then present your story to your partner as a tentative hypothesis, rather than an assumption about them, and initiate a dialogue that invites understanding and connection.

Why We Paint Our Partner as the Enemy

Why do we so often assume the worst about the person we love the most? When we're in a heightened emotional state, past painful events, insecurities about ourselves and others, and fears about the relationship can warp our thoughts. These are called **cognitive distortions**. And if we're not aware of and challenging them, they can pull us down a rabbit hole of fear, disconnection, and distrust. Here are some of the common thought distortions that show up in relationship conflict:

Mind reading: Assuming you know what your partner is thinking and attributing their intentions to your beliefs about them. Example: You stayed out late with friends and didn't get home until your partner was already asleep. The next morning, when they don't say much, you think, *They're trying to punish me. They're mad I stayed out too late, and that's why they're so quiet this morning.*

Overgeneralization: Drawing broad conclusions based on one example or little evidence. Example: Your partner is distracted and doesn't hear something you said. You think, *What I have to say doesn't matter to them.*

Personalization: Assuming everything is about you. Not realizing that while some things are about you, most are not. The way others treat you is mostly about them and what they have going on inside. It usually has little to do with you. Example: Your partner doesn't like the food at a restaurant you suggested. When they share their opinion, you interpret it as a reflection of the way they feel about you. You think, *They never trust my taste or like* *anything I pick.* Or if your partner is quiet, you ask what's wrong. They say, "Nothing," but you don't believe them and assume it's something you've done.

Shoulding: Believing thoughts you have internalized from childhood or society about what you're meant to do or not do in a situation, regardless of your own wants and needs. It's disregarding your own internal compass in favor of what others expect. Example: Your partner asks you to go to an event on a weekend when you're exhausted and overwhelmed and have nothing left to give. You tell yourself that you should go and force yourself to do it because you don't think it's okay to say no. To make matters worse, you come down with a cold the next day and then resent your partner for the whole experience.

Catastrophizing: Immediately going to the worst-case scenario or thinking the worst of your partner. A first cousin of jumping to conclusions, catastrophizing is very common with triggers and often generated by underlying fear. Example: Your partner doesn't call at the designated time. You envision them out having an affair or assume they're dead. Or you get into an argument and immediately start planning where you're going to rent an apartment when you get divorced.

Do you recognize yourself in any of these cognitive distortions? Think back to a moment of disconnection. What was the story you told yourself about your partner, their intentions, or your relationship in that moment? Did any of these distortions show up?

I've been guilty of most of these and *still* notice them cropping up from time to time, especially if I'm triggered. Don't judge yourself; it's normal.

You don't have to memorize all these cognitive distortions or prevent them from happening. What's important is to understand that they're common and will occur in conflict. But they don't have to undermine your relationship unless you let them.

The problem is not that you have these thoughts; it's that you can get so caught up in your thoughts that the Negative Partner Story takes over. You can't stop the thoughts from coming, and you don't need to. Just hold them lightly and allow them to come and go, like the surf, without getting overwhelmed by them.

Challenging Partner Expectations

Many of the expectations we form earlier in life are subversive myths, hiding like wolves in sheep's clothing. We create fairy tales about what our partners should do if they're good partners and really love us. Yet *should*s are always a lie. Any time something has a *should* attached, it's someone else's expectation that we've absorbed. That doesn't mean they're all bad or that all *should*s must be automatically dismissed. Rather, we need to scrutinize these outside ideas, decide which ones really serve us, and discard the rest.

Here are ten myths women often believe that interfere with intimacy, prevent them from taking responsibility, and undermine their relationships.

Myth 1: My partner should be responsible for meeting all my needs.
Reality: You are responsible for taking care of your needs, and your partner is there for support.

Myth 2: My partner should know how to meet my needs exactly as I imagine them.
Reality: No one is a mind reader. You are responsible for communicating your needs clearly in every interaction.

Myth 3: My partner should meet my needs exactly the way I want them met, or it isn't good enough.

Reality: It doesn't have to be perfect; effort is a sign of caring.

Myth 4: A good partner should do certain things automatically, so I shouldn't have to say anything.

Reality: Everyone shows love differently. You have to express what you need because your partner may operate from a very different script.

Myth 5: I've told my partner this before, so I shouldn't have to say it again now.

Reality: There is no way your partner can possibly intuit what you need right in that moment unless you tell them.

Myth 6: If I have to tell my partner what my needs are, then it doesn't count when they meet them.

Reality: Telling is the only way your partner can possibly know what you need. Their responsiveness is what shows their love for you.

Myth 7: If my partner really loved me, they would meet my needs just as I envision them.

Reality: Your partner may show love differently, and it's unlikely that this difference is a sign of a lack of love.

Myth 8: If my partner doesn't communicate well, then I don't have to.

Reality: You're responsible for upholding mature adult standards of communication no matter what your partner does.

Myth 9: It would be worse to put my needs out there and not get them met than it is to keep them to myself.
Reality: You have no chance of getting your needs met unless you're willing to take risks.

Myth 10: Expressing a need and not having it met is intolerable.
Reality: Even though it may hurt if your partner doesn't do what you hoped, you are an adult and can cope with it.

These are self-limiting beliefs that feel so true to the one who holds them that they're accepted unequivocally, driving avoidance like a giant turbine. Remember, these are the kinds of ideas we've absorbed from romantic tropes perpetuated by media, idealistic societal messages, and emotionally immature family members who influenced us as we grew up—they aren't accurate and they prevent us from speaking up properly in our relationships.

Which of these myths have you told yourself? Where did you learn them? Is there any payoff for holding these beliefs? What might these myths be protecting you from? What might these myths be blocking for you? Are there any myths that you would add?

The underlying secret is that these beliefs offer an insidious secondary consequence: They trick you into avoiding being vulnerable. They are justifications that make it seem desirable to silence yourself. They protect you from the immediate discomfort of putting yourself out there, but in the end they only hurt you. You have to reject them to achieve real growth and the possibility of connection.

These myths come down to one powerful emotion: fear. Being vulnerable and taking the risk to speak up can be terrifying. But if you indulge in that fear of self-expression, it will rob you of agency. These mythical expectations are like fun-house mirrors, distorting your relationship reality and justifying the choice to avoid. You may wind up being disappointed in your partner and questioning your own worth and lovability, when the real reason your needs aren't met is that you avoided the conversation and didn't put them out there.

Antidotes to the Negative Partner Story

Rather than defaulting to avoidant protective behaviors, you can take a pause to notice your thoughts and challenge them. Try not to attach too much meaning to them. You cannot possibly accurately interpret your partner's thoughts, feelings, motivations, and intentions in your own head. This is why you have to slow down, notice your thoughts with nonjudgmental awareness, and question them with curiosity and openness. By noticing your thoughts and reframing them in ways that are more realistic, you can get back into balance and operate from your Sage Self.

Several methods help with this process:

Noting, Labeling, and Reframing: This is a mindfulness technique to distance yourself from your thoughts and evaluate them from your Sage Self:

- **Note** when you are having negative thoughts about your partner and ascribing meaning that only they can define.
- **Label** those thoughts as distortions.
- **Reframe** the thoughts with perspective.

Imagine that your partner spends six hours immersed in their hobby on a Saturday, which makes them unavailable to work with you on an important household project. You find yourself thinking: *They should be helping me; they are so selfish; it's not fair; they don't listen; they don't care about my needs.* You realize you're creating a Negative Partner Story (Noting). You say to yourself, *That's interesting; I'm having distorted thoughts* (Labeling). Now that you have awareness, you get curious about your narrative. *Is there another way to see this? How might I evaluate this with more objectivity and balance from my Sage Self?* (Reframing)

Using a Mantra: A mantra is a personal statement, affirmation, or truism that you say to yourself as a guiding principle. Using a mantra to interrupt your thoughts and bring yourself back to self-connection is another helpful practice. This prevents the negative thoughts that feel true in the moment but are likely fleeting, from carrying you away like a magic carpet ride. Reciting a mantra, either internally or out loud, is a soothing reminder. It can help you separate from the Negative Partner Story and harness the perspective of your Sage Self.

Here's a mantra I've adapted from Kristin Neff's self-compassion work. I use it myself when I notice a Negative Partner Story developing in my mind:

I am having negative thoughts about my partner right now.
    Thoughts are not facts; they merely appear to be.
    Let me extend kindness and validation to myself as these thoughts pass through.
    I will determine my truth once I'm less upset.

This can be an incredibly grounding way to bring yourself back to the present and out of a spiral, where you can easily think yourself into getting even more upset with your partner than you were in the first place.

If you don't challenge your thoughts and instead just react, you may throw these distorted thoughts at your partner like facts, making them feel blamed and accused of things that aren't true for them. Then you're off to the races. This dooms your communication to fail and will condition the belief that things do indeed go badly when you speak up. But you can do this differently. Come to your partner prepared, knowing that the story in your mind is just that—a story. Just because it feels true in the moment doesn't mean it is.

Tend to Your Inner Child

Each one of us carries an inner child inside—the part of us that is most vulnerable, tender, and pure. Your inner child needs you to hear her, protect her, and take care of her just as you would an actual child. By connecting to and caring for your inner child, you will identify your core needs and be able to soothe and regulate your nervous system— and move forward with your partner, together.

Your inner child holds painful emotions such as fear and shame, unhealed hurts, and longings for love and security. She has needs for comfort, reassurance, and safety—and it is your responsibility to take care of her and meet those needs. Particularly in moments of conflict with your partner, it's essential to take care of your little girl.

She is easily activated by attachment bombs and desperate to avoid the same pain she experienced in the past. There's an old saying in therapy: "If it's hysterical, it's historical," meaning anything that really pushes your buttons likely has roots in the past.

To that vulnerable younger self, time is irrelevant. When something happens in the moment, it's as if the painful event from the past is happening in the present. A protective part of you comes out to shield your inner child the same way it did in the past. It often overestimates the threat and is unaware that you're now an adult who can handle the situation from your Sage Self.

When the protective part handles the interaction with your partner, it creates the very damage you're trying to prevent. In its zealous quest to protect you, it chooses avoidant behaviors that may have kept you safe when you were young but now only disconnect you from your partner and destroy your attachment bond.

Everybody has these normal reactions, but awareness is key. Initially you may not understand why you're triggered or what past event it's related to. Old wounds are not always accessible for recall; some are deeply embedded in implicit or unconscious memory. It's only upon closer examination and self-connection that you can find the correlation and access the hurting younger self that needs you.

Your task is to be more conscious when it's happening and comfort your inner child. Go inside and talk to her directly, either out loud or in your mind.

Every time you're aware of the protective urge and the hurting child, you're changing your brain and improving the way you function. In *The End of Stress*, Don Joseph Goewey explains that conscious awareness releases a peptide in your brain that extinguishes fear. This makes it so much easier to be intentional in communicating with your partner.

Once you pause to process your thoughts and feelings and allow space for deeply stored information to surface, you recognize how your experience points to your present needs. All the work to embrace your emotions and challenge the Negative Partner Story helps you identify what you need in the moment and give it to yourself freely. Knowing what's happening and that you can do something about it is encouraging. If you dig deep enough, you'll find the little girl who longs to feel safe and secure. You'll heal old wounds in real time by bringing her into the present and advocating for your needs.

When you were a child, you couldn't effectively advocate for yourself; it was developmentally impossible. If you didn't have an adult to help you tend to your feelings and needs, you had to keep them bottled up and protect yourself. But now you have the chance to speak for that child inside. You have the agency and capacity to heal yourself by parenting her with loving care in the present.

Building Secure Attachment Inside You

There is no relationship as important as the one you have with yourself. Women who are secure in themselves prioritize their needs and believe they matter. When their nervous system is activated, they trust their own reactions and give them the attention they deserve. They take a pause and get curious, stopping and listening inside for clarity, offering their inner child validation and compassion. This creates secure attachment inside themselves.

You can do this, too.

Secure attachment with your partner starts with secure attachment within yourself, which comes from how you take care of your inner child.

Your task is to listen and tend to your younger self—comfort her, identify her needs, and act on her behalf. That's how you create a more securely attached relationship between the adult you and your inner child. This builds self-assurance to overcome what held you back in the past.

It's critical to be intentional about how you talk to yourself. In those difficult moments when you're activated by a trigger, soothe yourself like a loving mother.

What's happening with your inner child is similar to what happens with kids when they have meltdowns. They really need love and comfort, but they're incapable of asking for it. As adults we still crave reassurance, and we have the ability and resources to communicate clearly for those needs. We merely have to tap into our Sage Selves to make that happen. Self-Connected Communication is about taking care of that inner child and letting her know she matters.

As you were growing up, if you received messages that your needs didn't matter, you were fed a heap of lies that likely caused you a lot of pain over the years. Were you accused of being weak or selfish when you sought comfort? Were you discouraged from expressing yourself because you might upset someone else? Were you rewarded for being a good girl and seen as virtuous for not needing anyone or anything at all?

Many of us were disappointed by adults who were too damaged or distracted to meet our needs, or even in some cases unwilling. Some may have been doing the best they could, but still our needs weren't met. We can't go back and do anything about that, but we sure as hell can prevent ourselves from failing that little girl who lives inside us now.

How to Talk to Your Inner Child

Your conversation with your inner child must be proactive and intentional. As you learn to parent her, you'll talk directly to her with messages of acceptance and compassion.

Take the classic example of a kid who skins her knee. When in tears she limps over to her mother, she may hear, "Don't cry. You're being silly; it's just a scratch. Get back out there. You're fine." While this is an attempt to help the little girl recover and move on, it doesn't accomplish what's intended. It doesn't make her feel better. It leaves her alone with her pain and invalidates her emotional experience. It suggests that her normal emotional reaction to skinning her knee is somehow wrong.

A helpful response might sound like this: "That looks so painful! I know it must really hurt. It's okay to cry. Let's clean it and bandage it up. Would you like a hug?" That's validation and compassion in action.

This is how you want to talk to your inner child in a moment of distress.

Which version sounds more like you? Regardless of what you've been doing up to now, you can adopt a new method of caring for your inner child with reassurance. Part of being an emotionally mature adult is knowing how to self-soothe. It takes repetition before the new way of self-validating takes hold, but thanks to neuroplasticity—the brain's capacity to change—it becomes a habit with effort and practice.

This isn't the time to be hard on yourself or hold yourself to a standard of perfection. Baby steps. Be gentle and patient as you learn to show up for yourself with intuitive wisdom and compassion. Your effort to tune in will make that little girl inside you feel safe and heard.

There are two steps to talking to your inner child during a pause: soothing her and getting curious about what she needs.

1. When you know the child inside is hurting, you tune in and soothe her.
   I'm sorry you're going through such a hard time.
   I understand why you're feeling the way you do.
   I'm here; you're not alone.
   I love you.
   I'm going to take care of you.

2. Once you've soothed the inner child, bring gentle curiosity to what she needs by asking the following:
   Does this remind you of anything that happened in the past?
   Has an old wound been opened up?
   What do you need from me in this moment?
   How can I comfort you?
   Is there anything I can do on your behalf?

This is simple but powerful because you're speaking directly to your inner child from your wise and loving Sage Self. When you're mindfully aware, you're connected to the essence of who you really are—your very best self.

While there are many ways to regulate your nervous system, this is one of the best. It's a game changer. When your inner child feels listened to, validated, and understood, she begins to feel safe and trust you. You're now the adult who will be there for her, perhaps the way no one has ever been in the past. Every time you show up for her, you heal yourself and build your confidence.

You'll be amazed at how even a few moments of closing your eyes, putting your hand over your heart, and talking directly to this younger self inside will help you feel grounded and centered. Then you can speak up on her behalf from your Sage Self and express what she feels and needs. You'll be better positioned to communicate effectively and less reliant on your partner's reaction. When you're connected to your core self, you feel free from trying to control your partner's response and empowered to stand boldly in your own truth.

Processing Thoughts and Emotions
Brings Couples Closer

In a later session, after Paul and Veronica had been working on connecting to themselves and each other, I was able to help Veronica pause to process her emotions, challenge her Negative Partner Story, and tend to her inner child.

We revisited the subject of selling their home. I guided Veronica to first process her emotions by noticing the sensations in her body.

"There's a pit in my stomach," she told me.

"What feeling goes with that sensation?" I asked.

"I'm irritated."

"As you sit with it longer, do you notice any other deeper feelings beneath that irritation?"

Veronica closed her eyes and sat quietly for a moment.

"I'm hurt." Her Sage Self was online and able to allow and observe her deeper feelings.

"If that pit could talk, what would it tell you?" I waited while she listened to her body.

"I feel alone and afraid."

"When you feel that pit in your stomach, your body is telling you that you are feeling hurt, alone, and afraid," I reflected. "That makes so much sense given the uncertainty around moving and how difficult it has been to talk about it. What's the story in your mind right now that goes with those feelings?" I began to lead Veronica into noticing and challenging her Negative Partner Story.

"The story I'm telling myself is that my feelings don't matter to him and I'm not as important as he is. He'll force me to do what he wants no matter what I say."

"Is there anything familiar about that story? Anything it reminds you of from the past?"

"Yes," Veronica replied. "It's the same way I felt in childhood when my mother made us move so frequently."

"I get that. Are you open to the possibility that your story about Paul in the present might not be as true as it feels?"

"To that little girl inside, it feels like absolute truth," Veronica told me, opening her eyes. "But when I connect to my Sage Self, the wiser adult part of me knows it's probably somewhat distorted. I'm open to hearing more about what he thinks."

By closing her eyes and connecting to her Sage Self, Veronica was able to note and label her cognitive distortion as such. Although it felt true to her inner child who had been dismissed and discounted by her mother so many times in the past, she was open to the possibility of reframing it and curious to hear what Paul might have to say.

"Let's tend to that little girl now and find out what she needs from you and what you might need from Paul, too. Close your eyes again and put your hand on your heart so you can communicate with her directly."

Veronica nodded and followed my instructions.

We all sat in silence while Veronica listened to her little girl. I glanced at Paul to gauge his reaction. He leaned in toward her and appeared totally focused. There was a look of openness and receptivity on his face that told me he was engaged and it was safe to proceed.

After a couple of minutes Veronica said, "The little girl says she's scared. It's happening again. It's just like all those times my mother moved us for some horrible boyfriend, and I had to leave my friends and start over. She never cared how it impacted me or paid attention to my feelings whatsoever. I was always alone with my fear."

"That must have been so painful for that little girl," I said, knowing that the little girl was now present in the room and listening to me, too. "What does she need to hear from you right now?"

"That my feelings matter; that I'm important; that I deserve to have a say about what happens to me."

"Yes! Of course she needs that. Can you talk to her directly right now and give her the validation and compassion she needs right in this moment?"

Veronica nodded that she could.

"Can you tell her that your Sage Self is here with her in the present and that her feelings do matter? That she is important to you and worthy of speaking up?"

Veronica sat quietly while she conducted this dialogue with the little girl inside. She let me know when that felt complete. I proceeded by suggesting she ask the little girl what she needs from her as it pertains to Paul.

"She needs to know that I will keep her safe by advocating for her. That she doesn't have to be a part of it. That my adult self won't stay quiet, but she can."

"Beautiful. Can you tell her that she has a say in her life now that you're here to advocate for her? Tell her that your Sage Self will communicate with Paul on her behalf, and no matter how he reacts or responds you will handle it and protect her."

Paul continued to lean in, watching Veronica hold her hand on her heart as a tear slid down her cheek. Eventually a peaceful expression came over her face, and she smiled, opening her eyes to return to the room.

"What do you need from Paul?" I asked.

"I need to know that my feelings matter. He doesn't have to agree with me, but I do need him to listen to me and validate that I have a right to my feelings. I also need to know that I'm important to him. I think I might need all of this more than I need to keep our house." She laughed, wiping her face with a tissue.

I was excited that her answer was swift and clear. All that work she had been doing to connect to herself more deeply was apparent and so different from when she first came to therapy and was blaming Paul for her refusal to communicate. Now Veronica was able to tune in to her emotions, hold her Negative Partner Story lightly, and identify what she needed from herself and Paul.

It was time to be curious about Paul's reaction.

"What's it like for you to hear this?" I asked him.

"I had no idea this ran so deep for her," Paul said softly. "I never want her to feel like she's not important to me or that her feelings don't matter. She's the most important person in the world, and I care about her and the little girl. I was afraid that she wanted to divorce me and just wasn't telling me yet. I mean, I really do want to move to the beach, but I would never force that on her. I'm willing to reconsider selling the house now that I understand what it's really about."

Veronica's vulnerable self-disclosure had made it easier for Paul to understand what Veronica was really feeling and to be open and responsive in return.

Veronica felt a surge of relief and deeply connected to Paul. She had taken a pause to regulate her nervous system, get clear about what she felt and needed to say, and communicate it with assertiveness, vulnerability, honesty, and kindness—the guiding principles of Self-Connected Communication. As a result, she got a compassionate response. Paul moved toward her emotionally instead of further away. She heard the reassuring words she needed in that moment—that she was important to him. He was willing to be responsive to her needs because she mattered.

Veronica had never before experienced emotional intimacy like this with Paul, or her mother for that matter, and by taking the time to process her thoughts and emotions and speak up about her needs, she reparented her little girl and created connection with Paul. Her husband's curiosity, openness to her feelings, and consideration of her wants and needs were healing. It was a corrective emotional experience that made her inner child feel safer and showed her it was actually better to address conflict than avoid it.

Paul would also need to process his thoughts and feelings and share them with her. If Veronica was as open and accepting of him as he was of her, they would have the emotional safety and connection they needed to move on to talking about a possible solution to whether they should move. With emotional safety, I suspected they could come up with a win-win solution—one that factored in both of their feelings and needs.

Questions for Reflection

- How do you feel about the idea of tuning in to and accepting your emotions?
- Does dealing with your feelings scare you or make you uncomfortable?
- Do you typically know what you feel in a given moment, or do you need a longer amount of time to uncover your feelings?
- Are you aware of any cognitive distortions or Negative Partner Stories that come up repeatedly?
- Is this the first time you've connected with your inner child? What have you discovered about yourself as a result of making contact with her?
- Do you find it challenging to offer yourself validation and compassion? If so, what gets in the way?
- How confident do you feel about speaking up for your needs with your partner?

PART III

Speaking Up in Your Relationship

≡

CHAPTER 6

Prepare Before You Share

The other night I spotted a distressing sight at my front door—
something that really challenged my Self-Connected Communication skills. It wasn't an intruder or a solicitor jamming the doorbell
on a mission to sell. It was actually my husband's dress shoes, cast off
when he got home and left to sit in our entryway like two haughty,
indolent cats. They mocked me with their refusal to live where they
belonged—the shoe bench (that cost a small fortune) was just two
feet away. *Why,* I asked myself, *are they sitting right in the middle of
our hallway, MOCKING ME?* Can you tell how much this pushed
my buttons? *Deep breaths.*

   I'm one of those people who can't relax in their home environment
until every single item is put away. I like my house clutter-free to an
extreme. It's not OCD, but it is related to anxiety. It's also a bit neurotic,
I'll admit . . . but I like to think a little dose of neuroses makes me more
interesting. I doubt my husband would agree. At times he finds my
standards stifling and feels micromanaged by my need for order. I get it.
I would probably annoy me, too, but I can't help how it makes me feel.
When those shoes sit on the floor assaulting my eyeballs with their ob-
trusiveness, I want to storm into the family room and go ballistic.

I've asked fifteen thousand times (my favorite number to quote when I'm exasperated) could he please, *please,* take the extra ten seconds to pick up the shoes? He'd tell you that he does that 90 percent of the time; I'd tell you it's 10 percent at best. But there is no objective truth, and it's pointless to go down that road. We simply have a difference that we must navigate. Although it infuriates me, I've started keeping my mouth shut because harping on the same detail again and again seems petty. I don't want to start a fight about a pair of loafers after a long workday. Plus, it never seems to change anyway.

A part inside me whispers: *This is silly. It's just a pair of shoes on the floor. Don't be a nag. It's not worth it. He'll get defensive, and then we'll spiral. Just suck it up, buttercup.* Although I feel the siren call to self-silence, I know that I'd be trading short-term discomfort for a long-term sentence in the cave of resentment if I give in to its sway. I know I need to speak up, but that doesn't mean it's easy.

I've been at this for a long time, but I still can't quite formulate exactly what I want to say until I've committed my inner experience to paper and had time to reflect. Whenever I'm triggered, I pause to process my experience, and then I use the Self-Connected Communication Blueprint—a series of writing prompts and questions that we'll learn about in this chapter—to help distill and clarify what's most important to share. This prepares me to approach my partner intentionally and effectively with the best chance possible that I'll be heard. And I'll tell you: It really does work.

When I took a pause and used the Self-Connected Communication Blueprint on this particular occasion, I found that my irritation went far deeper than the shoes. The Negative Partner Story was churning: *He doesn't listen. If he told me something bothered him, I would go out of my way to stop doing it. He doesn't care.*

Then I realized: The message that my needs don't matter took me right back to the wounds I incurred in my first marriage, when I felt like I was never heard or listened to. I also remembered that when I was in middle school and my parents were fighting a lot, I'd cope with distress by cleaning my room. I would fold my sweaters in perfect colorful squares of wool, organizing them by hue in my armoire to look like Benetton, the European clothing store that was all the rage among tweens back then.

Whoa. I suddenly understood. *This need for order is a long-standing coping mechanism that is much more about* me *than it is about my husband or his (cursed) loafers.*

By getting clear on what I wanted to say and writing it out, I was able to distill what I needed to communicate and effectively express myself. I told him, "When I see the shoes out on the floor, I get frustrated, but beneath that I feel hurt. It takes me back to my last marriage when I never felt heard. The story I tell myself is that you don't care about my needs. There's a part of me that just wants to swallow it because I'm afraid you'll get mad if I say something, and I don't want to fight. But this relationship is important to me, so I'm willing to take the risk to speak up. If you could reassure me that my needs do matter to you, that would help a lot."

My husband didn't get defensive this time. He was able to hear that it's about me and my past and not really much about him at all. He's not the bad guy, but I *am* upset when he leaves his shoes at the door. I feel a lot better when we talk about it openly, instead of keeping it to myself, even if nothing ever changes with the shoes.

Just as they helped me, the tools in this chapter will help you take whatever you discover inside when you're triggered and approach your partner with confidence and clarity. In conjunction with the pause, you'll learn to use the Self-Connected Communication Blueprint and the Taking a Delicate Dive tools repeatedly, whenever you find yourself percolating with that spiky charge of emotion that only your beloved can so effortlessly incite. These methods give you the best chance possible of being heard, creating connection from conflict, and feeling better inside yourself regardless of how well it goes.

The Self-Connected Communication Blueprint

In Part II, you learned to take a pause when you're triggered, to disrupt the false stories you tell yourself and instead connect to your experience inside. This is how you discover what you really feel and need. This process gives you the space to take care of your inner child before communicating with your partner out of misplaced frustration or anger. Now it's just a matter of putting it all together so you can initiate a safe, constructive dialogue with your partner.

Whenever something upsets you—whether it's a huge attachment bomb (such as discovering that your partner emptied out the joint savings account without consulting you) or a much smaller trigger (such as finding a sink full of dishes when it was your partner's turn to clean up)—you'll put the pause into action by going inward to process your emotions, thoughts, and core vulnerabilities. Then you'll write down what you discovered in the Self-Connected Communication Blueprint.

There is tremendous value in the act of writing. You don't have to be good at it, nor does it take a lot of time. The simple process of putting your experience on paper helps you regulate your nervous system. You'll start to feel calmer and more grounded as you let the words flow. When you commit your self-discoveries to paper, you're metabolizing your thoughts and feelings into something you can use, just like your body does when it converts a big dark green leafy salad into nutrients for energy and cellular repair.

Communicating off-the-cuff, in the heat of the moment, serves neither you nor the relationship. Once you say the words, they're out there. Forever. Using the Blueprint gives you time to digest what happened and mull it over *before* you engage with your partner. It guides you to distill your experience and obtain clarity about what you want to say *before* you speak up, and it becomes the road map for exactly what you'll share with your partner.

The Self-Connected Communication Blueprint

Now let's look at the blueprint itself and an example of how to complete it. If something is bothering you right now, you may want to use it to answer the questions as you go. Otherwise, simply read through and reflect on what you learned in Chapter 5 about processing your internal experience during a pause. Beneath each question I've included prompts in italics to guide you in your exploration.

1. *What was the trigger for my feelings?*
   What did you hear, observe, or sense from your partner that first activated you? It might have been an action, a facial expression, body language, your partner's tone of voice, or a combination of these. Write it down in concrete, neutral terms as if you are a fly on the wall observing the scene.
2. *What sensations am I aware of in my body in response to this trigger?*
   List any sensations you notice, such as heaviness in your chest, tightness in your throat, or a sick feeling in your stomach.
3. *What emotions have come up for me?*
   Begin with the surface-level emotions you notice, such as

frustration, irritation, annoyance, or anger. Write down at least one of these surface-level feelings. Then dig down into your deeper emotions. Is there any hurt, sadness, shame, or fear that you're aware of? Make note of at least one of these deeper feelings.

4. ***What is my Negative Partner Story?***
Your thoughts have likely fed you a distorted narrative of your partner or the relationship. What meaning are you making of what happened? What are you telling yourself about your partner or your relationship that feels true in the moment?

5. ***How do I want to protect myself with avoidant behavior?***
What does the protective part of you want to do in reaction to the trigger? What is your instinctive urge? Is it to ignore, criticize, blame, yell, or avoid in some other way?

6. ***If I could say anything I wanted to right now, without worrying about how it sounds or lands, what would I say to my partner?***
What do you really want to say to your partner right now? What would the protective part of you that is upset and filled with righteous anger, frustration, or irritation say, if it could run the show? This is your chance to rant—blame, accuse, make assumptions, stream-of-consciousness curse, berate, and let your partner know that it's not fair, they're wrong, and you don't deserve this! Whatever comes to you, write it down and get it all out.

7. ***What does this remind me of from the past?***
Float back in time and consider when you've felt this way before. Are these feelings familiar? Remember, if it has a charge, it has lineage, but it might have been a very different scenario in the past that produced similar feelings. Is there anything from childhood that comes up? Anything from previous relationships? Earlier times in this relationship? Write down anything that this attachment bomb reminds you of from your own history.

8. *What are my fears?*

   What fears do you notice having about the relationship in the immediate aftermath of this trigger? What are you afraid will happen if you speak up about this issue? Are you afraid of arguing? Do you worry that you'll jeopardize the relationship by addressing a difficult topic? Are you concerned your partner will get upset? Are you worried your partner will disagree with you? If so, what does this mean for you? List any and all fears you notice.

9. *Did anything happen that crossed a boundary for me?*

   Did your partner do or say something that violated your fundamental boundaries, such as using disrespectful language, yelling, or hurling insults about your character? Were there any actions that crossed a line? Often boundaries haven't been crossed, but if they have, it's important to take note and get clear.

10. *What does my inner child need from me right now?*

    What does the little girl inside you need? What does your inner child need to hear from you right now, so she knows you are with her and will take care of her?

11. *What do I need from my partner right now?*

    What do you need from your partner? Is it comfort and reassurance? Is there a specific behavior change you'd like to request from your partner? How would you like this type of situation to be handled in the future?

12. *What can I take responsibility for in this interaction?*

    How did you contribute to the exchange? Did you react protectively when you were triggered? Did you do or say anything, even something small, that might have contributed to the situation? If so, write it down. It's important to take responsibility for the role you played, no matter how minor.

13. *What might my partner's perspective be?*

Can you put yourself in your partner's shoes for a moment and imagine where they're coming from? What might your partner be experiencing emotionally? Can you hold space for the possibility that the Negative Partner Story in your mind may be at least partially wrong? Can you give your partner the benefit of the doubt in this instance? Why or why not?

Now pull from what you've written here and distill it into the following formula. This summarizes how you were impacted, including your feelings and needs, and provides a framework for what you'll share with your partner:

When I heard or saw_____
(what triggered you, stated neutrally)

I felt_____
(list all your surface and deeper emotions)

The story I told myself was _____
(your Negative Partner Story)

It reminds me of when _____
(times you felt this way in the past)

I wanted to protect myself by _____
(your protective urge to avoid)

Because I'm afraid that_____
(list all your fears)

I've discovered that I need_____

(your needs for comfort, reassurance, or behavior change)

The next time you're triggered by your partner, you'll take a pause and then use this blueprint to write out what you discover. Remember, the act of writing crystallizes the essence of what you need to say. It connects you to your Sage Self and ensures that you're empowered, confident, and clear before you engage with your partner.

Using the Blueprint

Stella proudly shared in session that she had been able to take a pause and use her blueprint after an attachment bomb went off with her husband, Pete.

Stella and Pete have been married for twenty-three years and have three kids: Ruby, a twenty-year-old sophomore in college; Burke, a sixteen-year-old high school junior; and Pia, a thirteen-year-old eighth grader. Pete runs a small architecture firm, and Stella has not worked outside the home since Ruby was born. As a result, they have an unspoken agreement that Stella handles the domestic domain and most of the day-to-day obligations with the kids. Values-wise they agree with this division of labor, and it seems to make the most sense for their schedules. Despite this, Pete sees himself as someone who contributes to household duties, often cooking and doing the dishes and the laundry. He does far more than his father ever did, so he believes he is a good, helpful partner and is happy to contribute.

Stella agrees that Pete helps with some things and appreciates what he does, but she often feels that he doesn't understand just how much falls on her plate and how time-consuming it can be. She bears the brunt of the *mental load*—the cognitive and emotional responsibility for running a household and caring for a family—not to mention executing the majority of the tasks. Even in these modern times, she believes there's still an unspoken bias against her for not having a "real job" and an expectation that she should do it all—a perspective Pete vehemently denies.

Leading up to the triggering incident, Stella had been busy helping Ruby prepare to return to college, getting Burke ready for school and football season, and shuttling Pia back and forth to gymnastics practice and orientation activities. Additionally, she's on the board of a local charity that builds homes for those in need, and she has been swamped with planning their upcoming annual fundraiser. Stella has been busy, stressed, and overwhelmed, more so lately than usual.

Last Saturday, the over-the-range microwave suddenly died. It's tough to go long without a microwave in a busy household of five. When Stella got home, she hadn't gotten both feet through the kitchen door before Pete asked her if she'd ordered the replacement yet. He seemed visibly frustrated with her answer. She hadn't had time, she explained, and then he walked off muttering something under his breath she couldn't quite make out. Stella felt a surge of anger and wanted to fire off a sarcastic remark but refrained. Normally, in the past, she would have ignored her feelings and pushed them down, waiting for them to pass, until the next time something like that happened, when it would all come rising back up again.

When I first met Stella, she had been living in the cave of resentment for quite some time, with many stored-up, unprocessed incidents like this trapped inside her. But now she knows how to pause, connect to herself, process her internal experience, and distill it into what's most important to share. Here's what she wrote in her blueprint after the preceding incident:

Stella's Self-Connected Communication Blueprint

1. **What was the trigger for my feelings?**

   Pete asked me if I ordered the microwave, and I was immediately triggered by that question. He had an annoyed look on his face and walked away from me muttering.

2. **What sensations am I aware of in my body in response to this trigger?**

   I feel tightness in my chest, a pit in my stomach, and a tingling sensation in my face, arms, and legs.

3. **What emotions have come up for me?**

   I feel anger and resentment. Beneath the surface, my deeper feelings are hurt, sadness, loneliness, and disappointment.

4. **What is my Negative Partner Story?**

   Why does everything fall on me? Can't he see what I'm going through right now? Why is it automatically assumed that I'm going to replace the microwave? Why can't he do it? He doesn't see me or care about my needs. He doesn't respect my time. I'm just thought of like hired help. Stella will do it. This relationship is not balanced. It's not fair!

5. **How do I want to protect myself and avoid?**

   I want to stay away from him and give him the cold shoulder. This part of me wants to avoid a fight. I'm mad, but I don't want to get into an argument over something as stupid as the microwave. He won't understand anyway.

6. **If I could say anything I wanted to right now, and not have to worry about how it sounds, or having to communicate like a mature adult, what would I say to my partner?**

   I would say, f*** you. You go order a new microwave! You probably have more free time in a given workday than I do, and if it's such a priority, you do it. You don't care about me or my schedule at all. You don't even see me. I'm sick of it! I'm done with this!

7. **What does this remind me of from the past?**

   It reminds me of when I was little. Everything was on me because my parents were working all the time. No one was dialed in to my needs. I had to do everything myself. I never felt seen or like I was a priority to anyone.

8. **What are my fears?**

   I'm afraid of getting into a fight because that will be unpleasant and disconnecting. I'm scared that I'll say something and he won't understand, and that will hurt more. I'm afraid that my needs really don't matter and that if I bring this up, I'll discover it's true. I'm worried that if I speak up, I'll say it in a way that is hurtful to him, or I'll say something I later regret. That would make me very anxious and uncomfortable.

9. **Did anything happen that crossed a boundary for me?**

   Nothing crossed an existing boundary, but I'm not comfortable with an automatic expectation that all major household projects will fall on me. It seems like that's what he thinks, but I don't know for sure, so I need to check that out with him when we talk it through.

10. What does my inner child need from me right now?

The little girl inside me needs to hear that her needs matter. She's a priority to me. She deserves for me to take care of her and advocate for her by speaking up and addressing this situation with Pete. However, I have no control over his reaction, so she needs to know that even if he doesn't get it, I do, and she's important to me.

11. What do I need from my partner?

I would like to hear that Pete cares about my feelings and needs, even if he doesn't agree with me.

12. What can I take responsibility for in this interaction?

When I was asked about the microwave, I was immediately frustrated, which probably crept into my tone. Then I became defensive about why I hadn't ordered a new one yet. I also gave him a dirty look.

13. What might my partner's perspective be?

I can imagine that from Pete's perspective I seemed stressed and short. He probably thinks he just asked a simple, neutral question, and I snapped at him for no good reason. He's probably confused about why I was so upset and doesn't know what to say or do. Maybe I haven't communicated enough about how I've been feeling lately or asked him for help with things that would alleviate my stress.

Here's what Stella distilled from the blueprint to formulate what she would share with Pete.

Stella's Blueprint Distillation

When I heard or saw him ask about the microwave.
(trigger stated neutrally)

I felt angry, resentful, sad, lonely, hurt, and disappointed.
(surface and deeper emotions)

The story I told myself is that I'm expected to do everything around here and my needs don't matter.
(Negative Partner Story)

It reminds me of when I was little and I often felt my needs didn't matter when both of my parents were working all the time.
(past times that brought up similar feelings)

I wanted to protect myself by shutting down and being cold until I got over it.
(protective avoidant strategy)

Because I was afraid that we would argue and get disconnected, and that I'd discover that my needs really don't matter to him after all.
(fears)

I've discovered that I need to know that my feelings and needs matter to him. It's also important to me that we have a conversation about household projects and our mutual expectations for how those will be handled.
(needs for comfort, reassurance, and behavior change from your partner)

After processing inside and completing the blueprint, Stella was grounded enough to reach through her fear and take a risk to initiate communication with Pete. She knew exactly what to say and used the guiding principles of Self-Connected Communication that you learned about in Chapter 3, sharing her feelings and needs in a way that was assertive, vulnerable, honest, and kind.

She told him, "When you reacted the way you did about the microwave, I felt angry. The story I told myself was that everything falls on me and you don't respect my time. There was a part of me that wanted to give you the cold shoulder because I'm mad and I'm afraid we'll argue if I tell you about it. But this relationship is important to me, so it's worth it to take the chance to be vulnerable with you.

"This touched on an old wound from when I was a child and my parents worked so much that I never felt like a priority. Underneath my anger, the little girl in me was feeling a bunch of deeper emotions—sad, lonely, hurt, and disappointed. It would help so much to know that you do see me and that you care about my feelings and needs."

Because of how she approached him, Pete didn't get defensive. He was able to hear her and understand her feelings. Once they connected emotionally and attachment needs were met, Stella felt better. They were able to have an honest conversation about household responsibilities, which led to an agreement to discuss specific tasks as they arise in the future. In this case, Pete offered to order the microwave, and Stella happily accepted.

While it may not always go this well, you have to remember why you're speaking up. It's not just about resolving the issue or obtaining a particular outcome. Even if your partner can't hear you, which we'll address in Chapter 8, you're saying what needs to be said and taking care of the little girl inside. This is true self-care. You are neither avoiding the situation nor blowing up in anger, and that's the Goldilocks of it—the sweet spot. You're taking care of yourself by sharing your internal experience. By taking the risk to be known, you reveal what lies beneath the surface issue—deep inside—where your hopes, needs, dreams, and fears reside.

Taking a Delicate Dive into Communication

Stella's success in communicating with Pete was partly due to the way she started the conversation. The manner with which you approach your partner is as important as what you say. For example, using a soft tone with a calm facial expression cues your partner that they're safe with you. This way there's a better chance that your loved one can hear what you're saying and respond from an openhearted place.

Dr. John Gottman's research on couples has shown that beginning a dialogue with a negative, harsh, or reactionary approach is almost guaranteed to fail, no matter how valid your complaint. He emphasizes the importance of using a "soft start-up" when you communicate with your partner.

I've adapted this into what I refer to as **Taking a Delicate Dive**. This means approaching your partner with intentionality using the following elements:

- Asking your partner if it's a good time to talk
- Speaking with a gentle tone of voice
- Using open body language
- Speaking face-to-face
- Reminding your partner of how important the relationship is to you

- Expressing your fear of communicating
- Using "I" statements and self-focused language
- Sticking with one topic at a time
- Using the guiding principles of Self-Connected Communication: assertiveness, vulnerability, kindness, and honesty
- Expressing appreciation

These are the nuts and bolts of initiating an emotionally mature and safe conversation. It's okay to be upset, but you can come from your Sage Self and prioritize connection over protection. You can be gentle, clear, and honest while expressing a complaint or need.

Here's an example of an *indelicate*, ineffective way to communicate: Imagine your partner put a red T-shirt in the wash with your white pants and they turned pink. Maybe they look cute, sort of, but you want your white pants back, of course, and who under the sun doesn't know that red clothes can't be washed with whites, for goodness' sake? How infuriating!

You say, "Why would you do that? What were you thinking? My pants are ruined! You never make any extra effort for me."

If you begin this way, you're almost guaranteed to get a defensive or protective response from your partner. This indelicate mode of communicating is intense and accusatory, and worse, it implies a deeper meaning about your partner's deficiency—that they never make any effort for you—that is sure to raise hackles. Frankly, even though I've certainly been guilty of saying things like this myself, if my husband spoke to me this way, the last thing I'd be doing is leaning in to hear more about his feelings.

You don't have to pretend you're not upset or bite your tongue, which will only breed resentment and put you back in the cave. Instead, you can take a pause to process your feelings, thoughts, and needs; write it all down in your blueprint; and then let your partner know about your frustration without blaming, shaming, or attacking. None of that would turn your pants white again anyway . . . and it would only make your partner feel bad and tune you out.

Here's how this conversation might sound by Taking a Delicate Dive:

"Hey, I'm sure you didn't mean it, but when I pulled the laundry out and saw that my white pants had turned pink, I felt frustrated. Deep down, I was hurt because I really liked those pants, and the story I told myself is that I'm not important enough for you to make the effort. I felt that way a lot in my last relationship. It's hard for me to say this to you now because I'm afraid we'll get in a fight, but I'm trying to be open about my feelings. This relationship is really important to me and that's why I'm making the effort to speak up. Like I said, I'm sure you didn't mean to throw the red T-shirt in there, and I appreciate you doing the laundry, but next time could you please be careful to keep the whites and darks separate?"

This is said face-to-face in an even, gentle tone. Taking responsibility for yourself means refraining from making assumptions about your partner and instead focusing on your own experience. Acknowledging your feelings allows you to get regulated and access your Sage Self. Reminding your partner of how important the relationship is to you can help to open their attachment channel, meaning that it reminds them of the connection and bond between you. Hearing about the relationship's importance can be soothing and may soften your partner from a protective stance into receptivity. Furthermore, expressing appreciation rather than blame helps your partner hear your request without feeling as if their character is on the line. Wouldn't you respond better to the delicate dive?

While this example may seem absurd, remember it's the little daily frustrations and disappointments that couples actually fight about. It's not really about the microwave or the ruined jeans. It's about speaking up when you're feeling unimportant to your partner *because* of the microwave or the ruined jeans. That's how you take care of you.

Sample Script for Taking a Delicate Dive

Now that you've written down what's important in your blueprint and learned the elements of Taking a Delicate Dive, you can make it explicit. Remember that it's important to stick to communicating about one specific thing that has brought up some feelings for you. You don't want to launch into a laundry list of complaints (pun intended!). If you address things as they come up, you won't accumulate grievances. It's easier to focus on the topic at hand.

Here is a sample script of what you can say when Taking a Delicate Dive. Adjust as needed and use your own words or whatever feels most comfortable for you.

1. *Something came up for me that I'd like to share. It's about me.*
2. *Is this an okay time to talk?*
   (If "yes," proceed to number 3.)
   (If "no," then:)
   Okay, when would be a better time for us to come back together?
3. *It's really hard for me to bring up something like this with you because I'm scared we'll get into a fight. Then we'd be disconnected and that would be painful for me.*
4. *I normally avoid talking about these things, but I'm taking a risk to be vulnerable about my feelings because this relationship is important to me. I want us to be able to talk about hard things.*
5. *You don't have to agree with me or try to solve the problem. I'd just*

like you to listen and try to understand my experience. That would
help me feel safe and connected to you.

This approach primes your partner to remember that the two of you are a team and meet you in a deeper, more connected place. You're taking responsibility for your side of the street, for what you *can* control, and behaving like a badass adult. When I use the delicate dive with my husband, I can see the part of him that was ready to mobilize into fight-or-flight shift into connection. It works. It just takes practice. Give yourself grace; let go of perfection and learn as you go.

Sometimes, however, no matter how assertive, vulnerable, honest, and kind you are, your partner still won't hear you. If that's the case, you won't proceed with more self-disclosure; you'll pause and agree to come back to it later. I suggest pinpointing a time that the two of you agree on and committing to following through.

If your partner is in fact open, responsive, and engaged, then you'll continue. You will open up about your feelings and needs with a short, clear message pulled from the Distillation section of your blueprint:

When I heard or saw_____

(state the trigger neutrally)

I felt _____

(surface and deeper emotions)

The story I told myself was_____

(Negative Partner Story)

It reminds me of times when_____

(name events from the past)

I wanted to protect myself by _____

(name the urge to protect and avoid)

I am afraid that _____

(name fears)

It would help me if you could_____

(express a specific need for comfort, reassurance, and/or behavior change)

If your partner makes an effort to listen and understand, express your gratitude:

It means so much to me that you're making an effort to listen and understand my experience. This makes me feel safe and cared for. Thank you for being a good partner. I know it's not easy to listen to stuff like this.

Don't overlook the last piece. As you've learned, it's hard to hear feedback from your partner, no matter how gently it's stated. If your partner gives you the gift of engaged listening, make sure to reciprocate with the gift of appreciation.

Nicole and Maddy: Learning to Connect More Deeply

When Nicole and Maddy started therapy, Nicole was convinced it would be impossible for her to open up to her partner. Nicole would get flooded, or emotionally overwhelmed, whenever Maddy, her partner of four years, seemed quiet or moody. Sometimes Nicole would just sense that something was off with Maddy, and that alone would trigger her. Nicole would often struggle to figure out what she was feeling, let alone how to communicate about it. Confused, she would retreat and get lost in self-doubt and rumination. Nicole would not share how she was feeling or divulge any of her worries.

This would leave Maddy feeling perplexed and anxious about Nicole's silent distance. She then pulled away in response, and the two danced warily around each other, disconnected and frozen with fear about how to address the tension between them. Neither one had really done anything wrong; it was just the ghosts of old wounds and fears coming up in the present. This can happen to any of us, regardless of what kind of childhood we had.

In therapy, both partners learned to connect more deeply to their emotional worlds and gradually began to share their discoveries with each other. Maddy insisted she had grown up in the perfect loving home, but in time she recognized that emotions were avoided and conflict was swept under the rug. Therefore, when Nicole withdrew from her, the only thing she knew to do was pull away more. Maddy was quickly able get in touch with her uneasiness, fear, and sadness and express those feelings to Nicole.

For Nicole, it was much harder. Over the months we worked together, she developed a relationship with the little girl inside her. She realized that whenever her partner was around, she would automatically feel as if she had to push her own needs aside. Nicole determined that this reaction stemmed from the dynamic in her childhood home. Her parents were often upset with each other and would retreat into silence. Her mother would lock herself away in the bedroom until Nicole coaxed her out. She would blame herself for her mother's distress, as children often do. Even at seven years old, Nicole knew she had to manage her mother's emotions.

Nicole used to feel too confused and fearful to approach her partner, so she would wait out those uncomfortable feelings. But now, after spending some time connecting to her inside world, she has realized that when Maddy seems distant, Nicole's little girl blames herself. She automatically thinks she'd better figure out what's wrong and fix it. Simultaneously, a protective part of Nicole gets angry at Maddy "for putting that on her" because Nicole no longer wants to be responsible for anyone else's feelings. A logical part of Nicole knows that Maddy is probably not intending this and that it's the past coming up, but the feelings are real and can still pull her in like quicksand.

Now her Sage Self recognizes that the past is over, and she no longer has to assume those old responsibilities. She can speak up about her painful feelings and have a safe conversation with Maddy that will meet her attachment needs, providing connection and reassurance. At first this was too scary to imagine, but when she takes small risks to share her vulnerability, communicating becomes more comfortable.

In session Nicole was excited to tell me that she was able to use her blueprint and Taking a Delicate Dive communication style to share the following with Maddy at home.

"Is this a good time for me to talk through something with you?" she began. "It's about me. I want to share something about my feelings because this relationship is so important to me. I want you to know what's going on with me, so we can feel connected. Bringing this up is really hard for me because it wasn't something that was safe to do in my house growing up, and I feel an urge to sweep it under the rug.

"Do you feel open to hearing about this right now?"

When Maddy nodded, Nicole continued. "Can we sit down and maybe you could even hold my hand? That would make me feel safer. Talking about this is really hard for me, but I know avoiding things creates distance between us, and I don't want that.

"When I see you getting quiet and distant, my perception is that it's something I've done. I get confused and afraid. It makes me want to protect myself by pulling away, but I know that will disconnect us, so I'm coming to you instead.

"You're not doing anything wrong; it's just that I used to have experiences like this when I was a kid where I'd have to figure out what my mom was feeling and try to make her happy. It reminds me of that and I wonder if I've done something wrong. It's an old instinct to blame myself. It would help if you could tell me what's going on with you in those moments, and reassure me if it's not about me."

Maddy was receptive and responsive to Nicole.

Maddy reported: "It helped so much to hear all of this. In the past Nicole would just shut down and seem cold and pissed off. I would have no idea what had happened. I'd have to wait for it to pass, while feeling so alone and confused. Now I understand that it's just old stuff coming up for her, and we can talk about it."

At first Nicole could speak up only in therapy, but with time she grew confident enough to discuss her feelings at home and ask for reassurance. Today, she and Maddy communicate clearly and stay connected when bumps in the road arise. This is what you and your partner can achieve by practicing Self-Connected Communication.

When it comes to approaching your partner, it's only natural that some of the attachment fear that lurks down deep may rise to the surface. It's extremely vulnerable to put yourself out there when you're unsure of the response you'll receive. Yet the cost of keeping it in is far too great. That only abandons your inner child and keeps you stuck in the avoidance trap with zero chance of getting your needs met.

On the other hand, Self-Connected Communication empowers you to speak up for yourself. The act of writing down your inner experience helps you metabolize your feelings, so your nervous system is regulated enough to approach your partner with clarity.

When you're connected to your Sage Self, you're calm and open. Even if you're upset, you still have the observing presence and distance from difficult emotions to be able to talk about them. You give your internal experience the attention it deserves and allow your feelings to breathe. With permission to feel what you feel and perspective, you're prepared to communicate constructively.

You Take a Delicate Dive into communication, knowing you're doing your part to start off on the right note, taking charge of what you can control and giving your partner the opportunity to know you better. You can't guarantee that they'll respond well, but you're taking care of yourself either way and exercising your power. That feels good inside you, no matter what you get back.

Questions for Reflection

- Have you ever tried writing things down when you were triggered? If so, was it helpful? If not, can you see yourself following through with using the Self-Connected Communication Blueprint? What part of it feels most challenging to you?
- Can you identify what your inner child needs to hear from you before you address a difficult topic?
- Do you typically make an effort to start a difficult conversation with delicacy? Or do you tend to prevent vulnerability by speaking harshly or by avoiding discussion altogether?
- Which aspect of Taking a Delicate Dive do you think is most important and why?
- What are you afraid will happen if the conversation doesn't go well?
- Can you think of a small thing that you could address with your partner to practice what you've learned in this chapter?

≡≡≡

CHAPTER 7

Empowering Yourself

On a sunny Tuesday morning more than twenty years ago, I was flying to New York to retrieve my five-month-old daughter, Charlotte, who had been staying with my parents for the weekend. It was the first time I'd ever left her, and I couldn't wait to be reunited. As we approached LaGuardia Airport, the plane banked, bringing the jagged, majestic Manhattan skyline into view against the cloudless sky. When I glanced out the window, the Twin Towers were engulfed in smoke and flames. Panic flooded my chest. I couldn't make sense of what I was seeing. Every head on the plane was turned left, looking out those windows, trying to figure out what the f*** had happened. *I should never have left Charlotte*, I thought. Somehow I knew that what I was witnessing was no accident.

We continued descending until the horrific fireball had disappeared from view. My heart pounded against the white noise of the cabin. Suddenly, the plane shot up like a rocket ship. For what seemed like an eternity we flew in circles over the Atlantic with no communication from the pilot. A fellow passenger announced that he had called his office and learned that hijacked planes had flown into the World Trade Center.

"There are other ones out there. No one knows how many yet," he said, monotone, his face gone pale.

All I can remember to this day was how quiet it was. No one uttered a word. It seemed we were all in shock and thinking the same thing. *Could our plane be hijacked, too?* I thought about never seeing my daughter again and started to cry.

After lingering in the air for an hour, we landed safely in Rhode Island. I had held my breath the whole time, thinking our plane might go down. There were news crews surrounding us with lights and cameras as we disembarked. I spoke to one of them and then walked like a robot to the closest airport convenience store to buy a pack of Marlboro Lights, even though I hadn't smoked since college. I sat down on the ground outside baggage claim and chain-smoked every single cigarette in that pack, feeling numb and detached from my body. I remember thinking, *I'll never get on a plane again.*

Compounding the trauma, I later learned of all the people from my suburban hometown who had died in those buildings. It was too much. This began a pattern of avoiding flying that would last for years. It made things challenging, to say the least, and even worse, it left me stuck living a small, fearful life. While it's understandable that I didn't want to fly again that day or in the immediate weeks afterward, by continuing to avoid it altogether, I whipped myself into an even bigger state of fear. The protective part of me that was trying to keep me safe admonished me not to get back on a plane, even though that was exactly what I needed to do. The irony was that if I had pushed through, I would have been scared at first, but it also would have gotten progressively easier with each flight until the phobia was squarely behind me. Instead, my avoidance exacerbated the fear. This same mechanism is at work when you avoid communicating with your partner.

Acknowledging Your Fear of Being Vulnerable

There's no doubt that fear will make a special guest appearance at showtime—as you're preparing to Take a Delicate Dive into meaningful conversation with your partner. The only question is, will you acknowledge your fear and work with it, or succumb to its inhibiting influence? You can harness fear and use it to empower you, or you can let it keep you from the connection you crave.

It's essential that you acknowledge your fear of speaking up, notice its attempts to seduce you into avoidance, and persevere in expressing yourself. Fear will tell you to do the opposite of what's in the best interest of you and your relationship. As you know, it sounds the alarm that vulnerability is highly dangerous and that you should avoid revealing yourself.

My clients often say, "I don't ask for what I need because it would feel so much worse to say it and get rejected."

Yes, it's scary to expose yourself when you don't know how your partner will respond, but in this case your evolutionarily wired attachment system is overfunctioning for you. The real short-term threat is minuscule compared to the long-term benefits of using your voice. But fear pushes you back into those old avoidant coping strategies so you can stay comfortable, no matter what the long-term cost. This is just like what happened when I started smoking again on 9/11. It would take me another ten years to quit for good, but not before I had sustained some lasting lung damage.

On the relationship front, the cost of an ongoing fear of speaking your truth to your partner is as great as lung damage—arguably worse. It can deprive you of the possibility of building a deeper connection with your partner. A healthy relationship requires the capacity to feel afraid and still reach for connection from that vulnerable place.

Your needs matter, no matter how big or small the issue, and they deserve to be tended to. It bears repeating: You are never wrong for feeling the way you feel, needing what you need, and wanting connection.

Every time you approach your partner, it's important to first notice any attachment fear that's lurking beneath the surface. Acknowledging your fear helps you regulate your nervous system and prevents reactivity from taking over. You set yourself up for success and bolster your confidence when you accept that your fear is normal, get curious about it, and acknowledge it as you communicate with your partner.

Here are some important questions to ask yourself about fear to help you prepare for uncomfortable but critical conversations:

- *Is there a protective part of myself telling me to avoid conflict?*
- *How is that part trying to help me?*
- *What's the absolute worst thing that could happen if I bring this up?*
- *Based on past experiences, how likely is it that the worst will happen?*
- *Even if communicating with my partner may not feel great, can I handle it if the worst happens or if the conversation doesn't go as well as I'd like it to?*
- *Is my inner child feeling scared about having this conversation?*
- *What does that vulnerable part of myself need to hear from me right now to feel safer about having this conversation?*
- *Does this current feeling of fear remind me of any times from the past? If so, which ones?*
- *What would my inner child need to hear from me if my partner doesn't respond well?*
- *Can I remind my inner child that this isn't the past, it is the present, and offer her reassurance that my Sage Self will be with her every step of the way?*

There are no right or wrong answers. There is only what's true for you. You don't have to fight fear, push it away, or pretend it doesn't exist. Doing so only intensifies the feeling. That's what happened to me with flying after 9/11. I was determined that I'd never put myself in the vulnerable, scared position I'd been in looking out the plane window that horrible day. So I didn't. The next Christmas I took a twenty-four-hour train ride to NYC with a baby to avoid setting foot on a plane. I passed up wonderful vacations that would have required air travel. I even had family in Hawaii (Hawaii!) whom I couldn't visit because I was *not* going to get on a plane.

Eventually, avoiding air travel became untenable, and I forced myself to overcome my fears. I was terrified, but I did it anyway. I let myself feel my feelings and took action through them. Although it took many flights to desensitize the fear, I grew progressively more comfortable until I was able to explore the world again with a sense of ease.

The same will be true for you when it comes to communicating with your partner. Your fear will begin to dissipate as soon as you take action. Doing it makes it doable. Every time you take the risk to share your emotional world with your partner, you change your neural pathways, redirecting the way your brain fires toward health and maturity. You gain confidence when you show your inner child that there is now a safe, loving adult who cares enough about her needs to speak for them.

The Empowering Effect of Expressing Your Emotions

Often it feels safer to avoid talking about emotions, but as we've seen, it comes at too great a cost to both your well-being and your connection to yourself and your partner. Not only is it healthy and empowering to notice and name your feelings, but it's also the primary way to build intimacy. The benefits of speaking up are twofold: You don't leave your partner guessing (which cuts down the potential for misunderstandings), and you create more opportunities for closeness and bonding.

Authenticity is what connects us. It actually takes *more* courage to feel your feelings—to sit through the discomfort and express them—than it does to disown, distract, and suppress them (all avoidant behaviors that make you sick). Without sharing our feelings, we can have no intimacy.

Some people are surprised to learn that sharing painful feelings is one of the most powerful ways we connect to other human beings. It strengthens our bonds and prevents us from feeling alone in the world. But remember that your anticipation of how your *partner* might react is not what dictates whether you share your feelings. You share your feelings because it's good for *you*.

It's not your job to manage how your partner reacts to your emotions. When it comes to sharing them, you're speaking your truth and exercising your power. Your truth is defined and stated by you, not by your partner's response. And when you let go of trying to control your partner's response, you're empowered to deliver a clear, direct, and kind message about what you feel and need without the responsibility for how it's received.

It *is* scary to speak up, but it's less painful than the damage that comes from swallowing your feelings or lashing out in anger and frustration.

There's no guarantee that your partner can or will hear you. If they haven't done the work to meet you where you are, or if they're afraid of feelings and disconnected from them, they may not know how to respond to you. As difficult as this may be, it doesn't prevent you from tuning in and expressing yourself. As an adult you must take care of your own vulnerabilities by tending to your feelings. And likewise, you can ask your partner for support, but it's not *their* responsibility to take care of *you*, either. Both of you are responsible for your own feelings. This is the key to an empowered mindset.

The Importance of Cultivating an Empowered Mindset

Your mindset is everything. It reflects the beliefs and values you hold about your relationship. Marcus Aurelius, Stoic philosopher and Roman emperor, said, "You have power over your mind, not outside events. Realize this and you will find strength." You cannot control what your partner does, but you can work on you to ensure that you show up and take responsibility for your side of the street in each and every interaction.

Cultivating an empowered mindset is essential to being able to use your voice effectively, become more securely attached, and enhance your own sense of well-being. An empowered mindset is similar to psychologist Carol Dweck's concept of a growth-oriented mindset, as defined in her book *Mindset: The New Psychology for Success*. An empowered mindset means:

- Taking full responsibility for your side of the street in relationship communication
- Being open to making mistakes and learning from them
- Focusing on the process of communication and giving your best effort (rather than aiming for perfection and a predetermined outcome)
- Being curious about both your inner and relational experiences and what you can learn from them

- Being open to feedback and criticism from your partner
- Seeing failures as opportunities rather than harbingers of shame

When you have an empowered mindset you don't see yourself as a victim but rather as an agent of change, with full responsibility for your actions.

Most of us know someone who always sees the glass as half-empty. No matter what's happening, they look at the downside or focus on the worst-case scenario. People like this have a disempowered mentality; things happen to them, and they view themselves as powerless to exert influence. They may be going through the same ups and downs as someone else, but their negative view of those events is what actually shapes their reality.

Years ago, I had a client whom I'll never forget. Simone came in because she'd been diagnosed with cancer. Although her prognosis was good, it was uncertain. She was middle-aged and single, and both her parents had died; she had only her cat for comfort. Yet this lovely woman had a better attitude toward life than I did. She didn't deny the waves of terror that came for her at times, but she didn't swim in them, either. She came into session talking about all she had to be grateful for; she focused on the small joys of each day; she meditated to be with her feelings as they came and went, visualizing a healing golden light flowing through her veins. Not only did she beat cancer, but she grew through her journey and inspired me to reevaluate my own way of reacting to fearful events. I still think of her often and continue to be inspired by her graceful resilient mindset and approach to life.

Sure, some issues we'll encounter are much worse than others. Death, illness, and financial disaster are certainly more difficult to cope with than stubbing your toe. But there are people who can reframe even the most painful events because of their positive, empowered mindset. Some focus on gratitude or find a silver lining that helps them see the opportunity to learn and grow in the midst of suffering. Others take a victim stance and get stuck in self-pity and inaction, blaming circumstances or others for why they can't move forward.

An empowered mindset serves individual development and strengthens bonds in relationships. It allows you to develop your emotional maturity, which is the glue of a relationship over the long term. The meaning you make of what happens in your life and in your relationship, and how you talk to yourself about your experiences, shapes your perspective and determines the quality of your entire life, not just of your relationship. Your brain comes to believe whatever you tell it—and the more you say it, the truer it becomes. The circumstances outside you, no matter how dire, don't define your life, but the way you interpret and experience them internally does.

When your mindset shifts toward growth, you're confident that your feelings and needs matter. You're more self-assured. You know that you deserve to speak up, and you understand that it's your responsibility to do so. You step maturely into being a good partner, knowing it's not your role to manage your partner's emotions. And from this place of inner strength and personal power, you will experience whatever your partner does that bothers you—whether it's getting defensive when you're trying to give them feedback, making an insensitive remark, or dropping the ball on their designated household duties—completely differently.

When you have a clear and accurate understanding of your responsibilities, you can practice Self-Connected Communication, empowering yourself and paving the way for a more securely attached relationship.

Chloe and Amelia Change Their Mindsets and Take Responsibility

Amelia's arms were crossed tightly, gripping her chest. I could hear the sharp intake of her breath to a tempo that told me she was furious. She had been frowning since she walked in and wouldn't even glance over at her partner, Chloe, who fidgeted with her purse on the other side of the couch and smiled at me nervously.

The couple were in my office on the heels of a recent attachment bomb—Amelia had just discovered that Chloe had been secretly getting Botox after they'd agreed it was off-limits.

Two years before, they had gotten into a rare argument after Chloe spent several thousand dollars on esthetic treatments without consulting her wife. Amelia didn't agree with cosmetic procedures on principle. She saw them as senselessly vain and a total waste of money. Chloe felt differently. To her they were essential self-care that buoyed her self-esteem. But because Chloe didn't want to upset Amelia, she had agreed to cease spending money on anything more than an occasional facial.

Rather than honoring that agreement, Chloe continued getting Botox regularly and concealed it from Amelia. Her rationale was that "it wasn't really that much money" and what Amelia didn't know couldn't hurt her—or their relationship. She had the wrong kind of mindset, one that was self-indulgent in rationalizing and doing what she wanted while avoiding communicating about it.

Now Chloe was beginning to see the flaws in her mindset and that she hadn't done her part in taking responsibility for her actions. As a result, the relationship was far worse off than if she'd had the difficult but necessary conversation in the first place. Neither Chloe nor Amelia wanted to fight, and previous attempts to discuss finances were usually shut down quickly, if not avoided altogether.

For many couples, fights about money are often really fights about differences in values, which can feel very threatening to an attachment bond. Amelia and Chloe had divergent beliefs about spending and saving. Their solution was primarily to avoid the subject. They pooled all of their funds and agreed to consult each other about major expenditures.

But Amelia's salary as CFO at a tech company was five times that of Chloe's, which created a major power imbalance. In addition, they had very different spending habits—Amelia had grown up in a family of modest means who were frugal with money, and she'd never really shaken the belief that money should be accumulated and not spent lavishly. Although she had been extremely successful, she was still thrifty. A proud saver, she was cautious with what she earned and favored spending out of necessity.

Chloe, a mental health therapist, had also grown up in a family with limited income. Yet her upbringing had been quite different from Amelia's with regard to money; Chloe's family had freely spent whatever funds they had, and even though they'd gone through some lean years, her parents had always seemed to figure it out somehow. Chloe's attitude in adulthood was to save enough to be responsible and enjoy the rest.

Chloe found Amelia's parameters about money excessive and stifling. Amelia found Chloe's spending habits frivolous and stressful. This fundamental difference in values was unlikely to resolve, but it didn't need to. Amelia and Chloe merely had to talk about it. With an empowered mindset they could shed their avoidant behaviors around money and confront these differences head on to reach a level of mutual understanding.

For Amelia the Botox betrayal wasn't really "about the stupid injections," but rather that Chloe had lied to her. This was a financial betrayal, which can be anything from secret shopping to siphoning joint funds into an undisclosed bank account. When it comes to primary romantic relationships, even lies of omission, whether financial or otherwise, erode a couple's bond.

Trust is built through micro actions of integrity and honesty that connect two people like a bridge. Each time your words match your actions—you're transparent when it would be easier to conceal, or you choose radical honesty despite fear—the bridge of trust is fortified. But whenever you withhold something from your partner, no matter how seemingly small or insignificant, you destabilize your connection by failing to take responsibility.

Betrayals like this are often motivated by the desire to do what you want without having to assert yourself and face your partner's potential disapproval. Amelia and Chloe needed to be able to talk about their differences and this recent rupture. Instead, they got stuck in an avoidant dynamic that was playing out in my office.

"Why didn't you just say something if the Botox was *that* important to you?" Amelia asked with a sharp edge in her voice.

"I wish I could tell you stuff like that. But whenever I say anything about money, you run away." Chloe began to raise her voice as well.

"Nice. You're gonna blame me for the fact that you spent a bunch of money you weren't supposed to and lied about it? Forget this! I'm leaving." Amelia began gathering her belongings.

"Wait, I'm sorry, please don't walk out," Chloe pleaded, her voice cracking.

I moved closer to Amelia and touched her arm. "There's a part of you that is so upset right now and just wants to get away. Is that right?"

She nodded.

"That makes a lot of sense to me. Can you help me understand what you're experiencing inside?" I asked.

Amelia shared her frustration and underlying fear. There was a part of her that wanted to flee, which was her typical coping mechanism in situations like these. This part was trying to keep her safe. If she stayed, she might get hurt even more. She could get into a bigger fight with Chloe or hear something that seemed too threatening to the relationship. This was what she feared and what the part of her that wanted to bolt was trying to prevent.

Amelia had been protecting herself this way since childhood. When her family fought, she would run to her room or to a friend's house to escape. She developed more of an avoidant attachment style and typically sought to shut down or get away from conflict to relieve discomfort. She thought she was securely attached in this relationship, but once she found out Chloe had been dishonest, there was a part of her that not only wanted to run out of this room but wanted to run from the relationship as well.

Amelia had been in two relationships in the past in which partners lied to her, one about exposing her to a sexually transmitted disease and the other about being in communication with an ex. Both situations had completely caught her off guard, and the relationships ended badly. This situation with Chloe pressed on those old wounds, bringing them back to life. A part of her felt like it was happening again, and her inner alarm rang out, *betrayal, betrayal, betrayal*, alerting her that she was in danger. In her system, the betrayal warning signal meant one thing—flee.

Chloe was also disconnected from her own source of internal power in the triggered moment, and instead of speaking up clearly from her Sage Self, a protective part of her was taking over. This part was appeasing Amelia, apologizing and begging her to stay. It was trying to protect both her and the relationship. If Amelia was angry and left, Chloe would suffer. The relationship could be in jeopardy, a terrifying outcome that part of her would do anything to prevent. This was likely the very same part of Chloe that had withheld disclosing her Botox expenses in the first place. Keeping the peace and prioritizing the needs of others, even at her own expense, had always kept her safe.

While Amelia's attachment style is more avoidant, Chloe is more anxiously attached. She felt secure in her last marriage until she was shocked by her partner leaving her for another woman. It understandably rocked her world. Ever since, she's had what she calls "trust issues." Deep down she's always worried that Amelia will leave her or that she herself will do something to push Amelia away. This fear may have played a role in her lies of omission. She also feels insecure in this relationship because of their income disparity. In session she is terrified that Amelia will leave the room, and thus the relationship. To prevent this, a part of her reverted back to appeasement, begging Amelia to stay.

Now the conflict-avoidant dynamic that played out at home was alive in the therapy room. Chloe fawned; Amelia fled. The more Chloe fawned, the more Amelia fled and vice versa. Both were trying to protect themselves from pain with their default coping strategies in the face of what felt like a threat to their relationship. But their avoidant behaviors were only triggering each other into a spiral of more protection and avoidance.

Fortunately their triggers were playing out in session, where I could help them pause, regulate, process, and then speak up (rather than avoid the issue) with Self-Connected Communication.

Once we had slowed down and explored their individual thoughts and feelings and I could sense that they were returning to a more emotionally regulated state, I began to guide Amelia to take a moment to connect with her Sage Self. This wasn't the first time we'd worked on building a relationship with this part of herself in session, so the process was already familiar to her.

"Can you close your eyes for a moment, take a few deep breaths, and then see if you can connect with your Sage Self—that wise adult part of you that holds your power."

Amelia nodded. Her breathing slowed.

"What does that part tell you right now about speaking up for yourself?"

"That it's important and I deserve to do it."

"How does that feel inside?"

"Better. Good. There is a part of me that's still afraid, but I can also feel the part of me that knows I can and need to do it."

"Is there anything your little girl inside needs to hear right now that will reassure her?"

Keeping her eyes closed for a couple of minutes of silence, Amelia then said, "Yes, she needs to hear that no matter how Chloe reacts to what I say, I will shield her. She doesn't have to be a part of this. I'm an adult, and I will handle it."

"Can you tell her that directly?"

Amelia spent a few quiet moments speaking to her little-girl self with compassion, and she let me know when she was ready to move on.

"How does the little girl feel now?" I asked.

"Good. She feels safe because she knows I'm with her." Amelia had accessed her Sage Self and connected to it enough to empower herself to communicate from a regulated, adult state. Once that happened, she was capable of being assertive, vulnerable, honest, and kind, knowing internally that she would take care of her inner child no matter what ensued.

I helped Amelia distill what she wanted to say and express herself to Chloe directly.

"I got triggered and felt overwhelmed, and it made me want to run away. I've been betrayed in previous relationships, as you know, and a part of me felt like the same thing was happening again. It was really scary. Plus, I'm shocked and angry that you lied to me. I'm also really hurt. On some level I'm afraid that if we talk about this right now it's just going to blow up into an even bigger thing and our relationship won't survive it.

But I'm willing to speak up because this relationship is so important to me, and I don't want to be stuck in that same old avoidant pattern."

Amelia had tapped into her inner power in the face of legitimate attachment fear and took the risk to respond with Self-Connected Communication. It wasn't easy for her yet, but through self-empowerment, she took responsibility and honored herself by speaking her truth.

I could see the tension dissipate in Chloe's face as Amelia shared her vulnerability and named her fear.

I helped her process and distill her internal reaction and then had her close her eyes and connect to her Sage Self, just as I'd done with Amelia.

Chloe reported that her inner child needed reassurance that she had a right to her thoughts and feelings, even if her partner disagreed. She was able to speak to that little girl directly from her Sage Self to self-soothe and access her power. Her Sage Self reminded her that she is an adult now and no one can take away her right to her thoughts and feelings, as the adults around her had done when she was a child.

Chloe then turned to Amelia and shared her experience.

"I got triggered when you wanted to leave. I felt really uncomfortable and afraid. I'm panicked that you might leave me because I made a mistake. A part of me wants to do anything I can to keep you in this room, so I don't lose you. I know I messed up and I'm willing to talk about this and own my behavior. At the same time, I'm scared and this is really hard for me. Can you please hear me out? This relationship is important to me too and I want to talk this out in a healthier way."

Amelia nodded, dabbing her eyes with a tissue.

"Yes, I'll hear you out. All I want is to talk about this in a healthier way and stay connected. It'll be hard, but we can do this if we do it together as a team."

This conversation between Amelia and Chloe is a great example of what Self-Connected Communication with an empowered mindset sounds like.

Over time with subsequent sessions and the willingness to practice at home, Chloe and Amelia learned to tap into their own internal sources of power so they could speak up, even when they felt afraid and were tempted to default to avoidant behaviors.

Through Self-Connected Communication their dynamic changed, and they were no longer stuck in the avoidance trap. When Chloe felt the urge to lie, she noticed that urge but took responsibility for telling the truth instead. This was uncomfortable, but she felt even more empowered by her ability to take this new action.

Despite these gains, the process for rebuilding trust took time, as it always does. Amelia was easily triggered by even the smallest suggestion that Chloe *might* lie and jumped to assuming the worst. The difference was her newly empowered mindset: She was clear that it was her responsibility to notice these triggers, manage them, and communicate with her partner about her feelings and needs.

One time, they came into session right after Amelia had opened the mail to find an exorbitant doctor's bill for a laser treatment that Chloe hadn't mentioned. Amelia noticed that she was already mad at Chloe for "lying to her" before Chloe had actually lied to her! Perhaps Chloe planned to address it on her own that evening, but in the moment, to the most fearful, protective part of Amelia, that didn't seem likely. She was triggered by the bill itself, and how it evoked the ghosts of lies past. However, instead of running with her Negative Partner Story and her anticipatory anger, Amelia noticed that she was triggered, paused to process her experience, distilled what she needed to say, and then empowered herself to come forward and speak her true feelings to Chloe.

She was shaking a bit as she began to speak.

"When I saw the bill, I was triggered and I assumed that you were going to lie to me again. I felt angry, but underneath that I was scared. A part of me also wanted to avoid direct communication and test you. I had the urge to wait it out and see what you'd do, but I knew deep inside it was healthier to come to the table and let you know how I'm feeling. I hope you can see that this is my sincere attempt to connect with you and do something different."

I noticed that Amelia's voice had grown steadier and stronger as she continued to speak. The act of speaking up—while understandably scary and uncomfortable—was creating an even greater sense of empowerment for Amelia, and it was palpable in the room. Every time you honor yourself by speaking up, your sense of empowerment grows.

Hearing Amelia's vulnerability and courage, Chloe was disarmed. She was not triggered by Amelia's revelation, in fact just the opposite; she felt an instinctive desire to move closer and deliver the reassurance Amelia needed.

Chloe connected with her Sage Self and empowered herself to take responsibility for communicating her true feelings. She admitted that she'd had the urge to lie, but also that she had firmly decided not to. Chloe was committed to telling the truth and rebuilding trust no matter how hard it was. She validated Amelia's feelings by letting her know that those feelings made sense to her.

"How did it feel to share that with Amelia?" I asked.

"It was scary, but it felt much easier than it used to. If this had happened even three months ago I don't think I would have been able to get the words out. I'm actually really proud of myself." Chloe grinned, and Amelia broke into a smile and moved toward her on the couch.

Not only did this openhearted communication rebuild trust between the two of them, but it strengthened their individual sense of empowerment as they came to believe and *feel* that they could relate to each other differently. They developed a muscle for these new behaviors, and with that came even greater confidence. They had clarity on what they were responsible for and committed to the sense that no matter what, they each had to do their part to speak up. Chloe and Amelia experienced the joy of connection forged through the struggle to speak up in the face of fear, and it inspired them to want to do it more.

Having the right mindset for a healthy relationship means taking responsibility for communicating our own feelings and needs clearly. It means we don't allow protection to take over, even when we feel the urge to resort to avoidant behaviors. We can understand and have compassion for our protective instincts and are aware these may stem from attachment, but we don't have to capitulate to them—we can choose to have an empowered mindset. This means being aware of our instinct to protect and choosing a more adult response. We take the risk to communicate clearly and explicitly, while giving ourselves permission to mess up and learn from our mistakes, knowing we can grow and repair. With this empowering mindset we know we don't have to be perfect. We simply commit to self-awareness, take responsibility, and do our best to show up.

There is no substitute for the repeated willingness to show up and communicate. Even when it doesn't go perfectly, it connects you to your own source of power and self-love. Just like Chloe and Amelia, the more you communicate, the more empowered you feel, and the more empowered you feel, the easier it becomes to communicate.

The Tenets of Relationship Responsibility

Where I often see people go wrong in couples therapy is in blaming rather than taking responsibility. It's important to shift your mindset from blame and frustration to curiosity and growth. It's easy to give when you're receiving what you want, when and how you want it, but much harder to do so when your partner's efforts seem to have waned. This is when it's tempting to slip into a protective stance and avoid.

You have to change your understanding of what a relationship looks like to cultivate something healthy on honest terms. You focus on what you can control, do what you're responsible for, and let the rest go. It's not about your ego or being right; it's about putting pride aside to nurture the relationship. When you come from a place of confidence and clarity about your own responsibilities, you're able to maximize the possibility of participating in a mature relationship.

The following tenets offer a guide that allows you to care for yourself and tend to your relationship. When you take responsibility, these statements feel true in your relational dynamic:

- I am responsible for taking care of myself.
- It is my job to nurture my self-esteem.
- I am not responsible for managing my partner's feelings.
- My partner is not responsible for managing my feelings.
- How I react and behave is about me and not my partner.
- How my partner reacts and behaves is about them and not me.
- I am responsible for communicating my feelings and needs clearly.
- My partner is responsible for communicating their feelings and needs clearly.
- I take ownership when I've hurt my partner and make amends for it.
- I am the only person who can speak for what I think, feel, and need.
- My partner is the only person who can speak for what they think, feel, and need.
- My needs matter. Always.

TAKE A MOMENT TO REFLECT

- How many of these beliefs do you hold?

- Using a scale of 1 to 10, with 10 being completely true and 1 being not true at all, put a number next to each item on the list to reflect how true these statements feel at this time.

- Do some of these beliefs feel true until you're triggered? Which beliefs do you abandon when you're upset?

- In moments of conflict, do you have trouble remembering the ones you believe in and operating accordingly?

Your mind believes whatever you consistently tell it. Copy these tenets into your notebook and repeat them to yourself daily. In about a month reassess how true these statements feel on a scale of 1 to 10. If you stick with this exercise regularly, you'll notice a difference. As you continue with it over time, coupled with actions such as speaking up when you're tempted to avoid, you'll transform your old wiring into new beliefs that serve you in taking care of your emotional needs and speaking up for them with confidence.

To take responsibility you must draw on the strength of your Sage Self to tap into your self-worth and resilience. You have attachment needs for comfort, support, and knowing that you matter. It's natural to want this from your relationship, as discussed in Chapter 3. If your partner isn't responding and meeting those needs, it's disappointing, but when you take care of yourself you know you'll be okay. You can *always* give yourself the validation and compassion you deserve.

What You're Responsible For

Any time you are frustrated, hurt, or feeling pain, it is your responsibility to make sense of your feelings and to communicate them to your partner without attacking, accusing, blaming, or shaming them for upsetting you. Your partner's behavior may have triggered you, but they're not responsible for your internal emotional experience of that trigger. You are.

For example, in session my client Arielle got triggered when her partner, Joe, disagreed with her. She was explaining how her son's teacher had mistreated him. She immediately launched into accusations instead of taking responsibility for her emotional experience.

"I don't like how Daniel's teacher picks on him in class," she said.

"I don't see it that way," Joe remarked. "Daniel's a handful, and I think his teacher is actually pretty patient with him."

"Why do you always have to challenge me? Can't you ever just agree with me on anything?" she jumped in.

"What? I was just sharing my opinion, jeez," Joe said, sounding frustrated and getting defensive, too. "Can't we disagree without getting in a fight?"

Joe's comment had triggered Arielle, but her interpretation of the trigger and defensive reaction to it was more the product of her own past experiences and insecurities than about what Joe said.

Arielle grew up with a father who constantly critiqued her—on everything from her grades to the way she cleaned her room. He was a military man who thought the best way to prepare his daughter for life was to hold her to impossibly high standards and question her insights so she would learn to prove herself in a tough, unforgiving world. But his approach made Arielle feel like she wasn't smart enough, a belief she still hadn't fully shed today. As a result, she interpreted Joe's comment as evidence that she was stupid in his eyes and immediately got defensive.

If Arielle could pause to tune in to her emotions, challenge her Negative Partner Story, and tend to her inner child, she could take responsibility for her experience of the trigger and ask for what she really needed: to hear that Joe didn't see her as stupid and respected her opinion even when he disagreed.

Similarly, if you believe that your feelings don't matter, you might interpret your partner's silence as a sign that they don't care about you, instead of what it really is—their fear of saying the wrong thing. It's critically important to give your partner the benefit of the doubt until you definitively know otherwise.

Remember, nothing is as personal as it seems. What you experience emotionally is about you. What your partner experiences emotionally is entirely about them. Only you can speak for what you think, feel, and need; the same goes for your partner. And no matter how your partner behaves, you're responsible for taking care of your side of the street by doing the following:

- Tuning in to your internal experience to bring awareness
- Processing your internal experience and regulating your emotions
- Approaching your partner to communicate clearly and vulnerably
- Tending to your emotional needs with compassion

Your partner is not there to solve your problems, make negative feelings disappear, or do what you want them to do. They are there to be your secondary support. You are responsible for being a good steward of your own emotional needs and communicating them clearly.

Not only do you have a responsibility to your relationship to speak up, but you have a responsibility to yourself.

Sending Clear Signals

Telling each other what you're experiencing emotionally is like using the turn signal on your car. Have you ever been behind someone who's driving well below the speed limit? It can be so frustrating. On the other hand, when a car is going maddeningly slow but has their signal on, you have information about their behavior that mitigates your confusion. They're about to turn or they're trying to figure out where to turn. Maybe they're from out of town and they don't know their way around; maybe they're lost. You may still feel frustrated, but the signal assures you that there's a *reason* for the slow driving, and that helps you relax a bit. With information, it's easier to have empathy and patience. The brain hates uncertainty.

In relationship communication, you have to take responsibility and use your signal. When you speak up about what's happening inside, your partner doesn't have to guess. Not only is this good relationship etiquette, but it vastly minimizes the potential for misunderstandings.

For example, imagine you had a terrible day at work and come home feeling irritable, not wanting to talk or interact. Your partner sees that something is wrong the minute you come in. You have a scowl on your face. You are short and terse when they ask what you feel like having for dinner. You immediately get on your phone to doomscroll in an attempt to decompress. You don't say anything about your inner state of being, so your partner is left to interpret your behavior on their own. *Did they have a bad day? Should I leave them alone? Maybe I should just keep my mouth shut. It's probably something I did wrong.* Confused by your silence, they distance themself and disconnection ensues.

When you take responsibility and "use your signal," you let your partner know simply and clearly that you're having one of those days where you're exhausted and just need some time to yourself. Chances are your partner will happily comply, feeling relieved that it has nothing to do with them.

Responsible adult partners don't send mixed signals. They don't leave their partner struggling to figure them out. It feels much better when both parties know what's going on with each other. You can't overcommunicate.

Knowledge provides comfort. Give your partner this courtesy. You can save yourself from arguments and get your needs met much more easily. It is 100 percent possible to communicate clearly, but it takes intentionality, consistency, and connecting to yourself more deeply, as we'll continue to explore in the next chapter.

Setting Boundaries

Setting boundaries is an essential component of relationship responsibility and self-empowering. It's not about calling your partner out, telling them they're wrong, or trying to get them to do something different. You're not trying to force your partner to do what you want them to do. You're letting them know what you will and will not accept, and what you will do if they continue with behavior that is unacceptable to you. It's not a threat. It's an honest statement about how you will take care of yourself, so your partner can evaluate their own decisions and boundaries accordingly. Think of setting a boundary as building a guardrail around your inner child that keeps her safe from harm. Boundaries fuel self-worth, autonomy, and agency. They allow both your self-esteem and your relationship to flourish.

Since we're taught to be nice and be "good girls," boundaries can feel uncomfortable and downright wrong even though they're oh so right. We may fear that if we set limits, we will alienate our partners and jeopardize our attachment bonds, but it's actually the opposite. Boundaries are clear guidelines that make connection possible.

Christa Sets a Boundary

Here's an example of how my client Christa set a much-needed boundary in her relationship:

Christa has a partner who loses his temper. Dave yells and sometimes hurls insults; it has never gotten physical, but it gets ugly. Christa's father had a terrible temper, too, so in her younger years she thought it was just "what men do" and tried to accept it. Now at fifty-five, she's no longer willing to be silent, stuff down her feelings, or slink away in terror. But Christa believes that it isn't safe to engage or be vulnerable when Dave behaves this way, so she had to set boundaries to take care of herself.

The last time Dave lost his temper was over a misunderstanding about discontinuing their gym membership. Somehow it escalated quickly, with Dave bringing up a host of past grievances that he had stored up against her.

"I'm so sick of how you harp on me for every damn dish I leave in the sink. You're never happy with anything I do," he said. "You're cold and nasty! And we never have sex anymore, either!"

Christa called a time-out. Even though he had agreed to a time-out policy in which they would take thirty minutes to self-soothe before reengaging, Dave didn't respect it and followed her into the other room to yell some more.

She removed herself and went for a walk to get some space. She took a pause on her walk to self-soothe, process her experience, and get clear about what she needed. Christa discovered that underneath her anger she was scared, lonely, sad, and hurt.

This behavior had been going on for a long time, and it wasn't okay with her anymore. She had tried begging Dave to stop berating her, but he hadn't. She realized she couldn't make Dave change, but she could control how *she* responded to his behavior, and she could set limits to take care of herself. If he wasn't going to work on his temper and make an effort to behave differently, Christa would leave the relationship.

It was both scary and exhilarating to realize what was true for her— that while she still loved Dave, she wasn't willing to stay in a relationship in which she was treated that way. Her mother's recent premature death had made her more aware than ever of how quickly life slips by.

Christa and Dave didn't have children, and she was financially independent, so she didn't have those barriers to consider. Plus, every time he lost his temper, yelled, and insulted her, a little bit of her love for him died.

Christa didn't feel quite ready to initiate a discussion with him, so she decided to wait. The next day Dave went back to normal, acting as if nothing had happened. He didn't apologize or make any attempt to repair. At one point this would have hurt her deeply, but after so many years of this she felt somewhat detached and indifferent.

Christa approached him after dinner and told him she would like to share something about herself and asked if it was a good time. When he nodded, she continued with a simple, calm boundary statement.

"When you lost your temper yesterday, I felt afraid. I don't feel scared of you physically, but I do feel emotionally unsafe, and that's not okay with me. When you speak to me that way, I can't open up to you and have to remove myself. I'm no longer willing to live this way. I can't control what you do, but I want to let you know where I stand. I've reached the point that if that behavior continues, I will have no choice but to end the relationship."

Christa wasn't threatening Dave or expecting that anything would change. She had listened to the little girl inside her, the one who grew up in a home with yelling and chaos and would not let her live that way any longer.

Dave told her he had decided to go to individual therapy. He also asked her to go to couples therapy, and she agreed. She was willing to work on it, but if he continued to lose his temper, she would walk away and be at peace with it, knowing she had given it her all and been clear and direct in disclosing her personal boundary.

In Christa's case the lack of emotional safety was a cost too great to bear. She had spoken up and declared boundaries that honored her needs. She was assertive and honest in letting Dave know what she would and wouldn't do if his behavior didn't change. She wanted a partnership that provided emotional intimacy. If he couldn't manage his temper, she would be better off ending the relationship because it couldn't offer her the intimacy she craved.

How to Set Boundaries

Only you can decide when and where boundaries need to be set. To determine your boundaries, you must listen to your intuition. It's essential to identify the need that each boundary serves. They should be specific and centered on self-care.

Start by getting curious about your reaction to your partner's behavior and ask yourself the following:

- *How does my partner's behavior impact me?*
- *How do I want to protect myself?*
- *How is my inner child feeling?*
- *What does my Sage Self know about this?*
- *How would creating a boundary help me? What need would it fulfill?*
- *If my partner's current behavior continues, how will I take care of myself?*

Once you're clear about what you need, you'll be able to define your boundary. Then you can communicate it from your Sage Self. Just like Christa, you'll let your partner know what specific behavior is not okay with you, how it impacts you, and what you'll do to take care of yourself if it continues.

Here are a few examples of what you might say when you're setting a boundary:

- "When you shut down, it's not okay with me. It makes me feel unsafe and alone. If you continue to shut down every time I open up, I won't be able to share my feelings and needs with you. I don't know what kind of impact this will have on our relationship over the long term."
- "It's not okay with me that you get defensive when I'm trying to share my feelings. I feel hurt and disconnected when that happens. If you continue to get defensive, I'll end the conversation. I'm not going to continue to try to be close to you and share my feelings if you're not willing to listen."
- "When you make sarcastic comments after I open up, I feel hurt and angry. It's not okay with me. If you continue, I will remove myself until we can both talk respectfully."

Setting boundaries like this indicates that you respect and care about yourself. Just like you wouldn't let your five-year-old eat three sheets of cookies or step out into traffic, you won't let yourself or your inner child be harmed. You set limits from your Sage Self because you're worth it, and because it's your responsibility to look out for yourself.

In relationships it's essential to communicate boundaries clearly. Otherwise you're expecting something from your partner they can't possibly deliver. When you don't communicate your boundaries, you unfairly shift your responsibility onto your partner's shoulders, doom them to fail, and disempower yourself.

Connect to Your Power!

When you connect to yourself, you connect to your power. It's like putting a plug into an outlet to access electricity. You light up. Once you learn how to access it, no one can take it away from you. With an empowered mindset you set boundaries because you're willing to act in the face of fear and step into your responsibility, even when it feels most challenging and uncomfortable.

As you choose to speak up rather than avoid, your sense of empowerment grows. Eventually you'll look back and wonder how you ever tolerated doing it the avoidant way.

Questions for Reflection

- When you think of empowering yourself to speak up, what obstacles come to mind?
- Have you experienced how connecting it is to share painful emotions?
- What do you envision being the greatest benefit of taking responsibility to speak up and sending clear signals to your partner?
- Have you faced challenges with setting boundaries in the past?
- What words of wisdom do you need to hear from your Sage Self in the moment to empower yourself to follow through with setting and communicating boundaries to your partner?

CHAPTER 8

Dealing With Your Partner's Response

Monique and Ryan had been dating for three years when they came into therapy to work on their communication skills. They didn't have any major problems; they were totally in love and committed to each other, and they had similar values and goals. In fact, life was pretty good: They both had great jobs they loved—Monique as a Pilates instructor with her own studio and Ryan as an IT engineer and CEO of a consultancy firm. They had many like-minded friends, an active social life, and a golden retriever named Zukki they both doted on. Monique and Ryan frequently traveled the world together, having exotic adventures such as a safari in Botswana and scuba diving in New Zealand.

But when there was a problem of any kind, they got stuck in bickering loops very quickly. Monique tended to criticize, and Ryan often got defensive. When they first came in to see me, they had no idea what most of their fights were about or how they became so incendiary.

"Why did you keep turning the AC down so low?" Monique asked.

"I barely touched it," Ryan said.

"I've told you I'm freezing in here and you don't seem to care," Monique fired back.

"Well, you don't seem to care that I'm sweating through my shirt before I get to work!"

"It's all about you, isn't it?"

"No! You're the one who's always complaining!" Ryan countered.

And they were off—it didn't matter if it was the AC, whose turn it was to walk Zukki, or how much they should spend on their next trip—all roads led to the same types of bickering loops that they couldn't resolve.

Through counseling they discovered that their arguments stemmed more from *how* they communicated than what they were trying to say. They learned to take responsibility for their triggers, pause to process their internal experiences, and come forward to address, share, and repair. They were feeling closer than ever, and more and more confident about their ability to navigate conversations as a team. But these healthy behaviors were still new; even though they were having some success, they still got stuck sometimes, too.

One morning, Monique and Ryan came into session, sharing a sticky situation that had challenged their ability to respond to each other instead of reacting. Monique felt uncomfortable that Ryan was following his female coworkers on social media, often liking and commenting on their posts. The other night, she said, she'd come up behind him to show him a new travel spot in Indonesia. Monique found Ryan on his phone, liking a photo of his colleague Amanda, who happened to be super fit—and single. Amanda was in a bathing suit, sitting on a boulder next to some guy, grinning happily.

The threat was so triggering for Monique that her whole body flashed white hot. It felt like a freight train barreling through her veins. She had the urge to attack but caught herself and shifted into Self-Connected Communication. Monique left the room, took a pause to process her feelings, and distilled what she needed to say. Then she approached Ryan gently and asked if it was a good time to talk. When he indicated it was, she communicated clearly from her Sage Self, sharing her feelings openly and with total vulnerability.

"Ryan, when I discovered that you were liking Amanda's post on Instagram, it hurt and scared me. It felt like a threat to our relationship. The story I told myself was that I'm not good enough and that you find her more attractive than me. It's really scary for me to share this with you, and I hope you can see the risk I'm taking to open up because of how important our relationship is to me. I know some of this comes from my own insecurities and wounds from being cheated on in the past, but I'm also not comfortable with that type of online engagement with other women. I would like to talk openly about our mutual boundaries. But first and most important, I need reassurance that you love me and that I'm enough for you."

Instead of responding with validation and empathy, Ryan reacted heatedly and defensively.

"What? Of course I love you, but you're being ridiculous! Amanda's a friend from work. She's with her new boyfriend in the picture, for god's sake! It's harmless. I'm not going to be accused when I did nothing wrong. You're just trying to control me!"

Monique was hurt and deeply disappointed by Ryan's reaction. She had taken great care to communicate in a healthy adult fashion, but she still wasn't able to get through to him. She soothed her inner child and reminded herself that even though Ryan couldn't be there for her in that moment, her Sage Self could and would. Monique felt powerful and proud of herself for taking the risk to speak up. And she was determined to explain exactly how his words impacted her.

"I'm hurt and disappointed that you can't hear what I'm sharing. When you react that way, I feel alone and disconnected. I'll have to take some time to think about this and where my own boundaries sit, because I'm not okay with what's happening."

Monique knew that Ryan's response said more about him than it did about her. While it might not mean he didn't care, it sure felt like that in the moment. Still, Monique knew she was right in saying something, even if Ryan wasn't able to be there for her at that time. She wasn't comfortable with his social media behavior and wouldn't pretend to be. Even though Ryan's reaction stung, it felt empowering to come forward and speak up for her feelings and needs.

In this case, Ryan was too triggered and stormed off. But with some time to settle down and reflect, he returned and initiated a repair.

"I'm sorry I got so defensive. I felt like you were attacking me, and I wasn't able to listen. But that wasn't fair to you at all. I care about your feelings and want to understand you better. Can we try again? I promise to listen this time."

"What was that like for you when Ryan came back to repair?" I asked Monique in session.

"It was amazing. My anger pretty much melted away. Hearing him say he cared about my feelings, wanted to understand, and then offering me a genuine apology for how he reacted meant so much to me. We were able to talk it through, and once Ryan understood my feelings he told me he wouldn't like Amanda's posts anymore. He's still gonna follow her because they're friends, but he said he's happy to refrain from liking and commenting on her stuff to honor my feelings."

She looked down and shook her head slightly.

"It may sound silly, but his willingness to make changes made me feel loved and cared for. I don't even care about Amanda anymore."

It didn't sound silly at all. Monique and Ryan had made significant progress. They were committed to Self-Connected Communication and knew that while it wouldn't always go perfectly, they could each stick to doing their part—even when they didn't get the response they were hoping for. They could always come back to repair when their communication went astray.

What to Do if Your Partner Reciprocates

Self-Connected Communication works surprisingly well most of the time. Your partner likely wants to connect with you, too. When you lead with a soft tone of voice and attachment language such as "This relationship is important to me," you disarm your partner's protective parts into realizing that they don't need to mobilize an avoidant defense. You're doing your part to signal that it's safe to engage with you.

This approach works for a few reasons. For one thing, it activates our mirror neurons—areas of the brain that allow us to mimic and replicate what we see. We naturally learn, empathize, and understand by syncing with others' body language, facial expressions, and behavior.

Authenticity also softens the receiver. When you're vulnerable and genuine, you invite your partner to do the same. Sharing your struggles and hardships allows your partner to feel more comfortable opening up. They're less likely to avoid or protect themself when you approach with arms wide open, no weapons in sight. When you feel heard and accepted, your entire body exhales in relief.

Connection flourishes when your partner meets you in emotional vulnerability and comes alongside your experience with an outstretched hand. If your partner meets you in that place, reciprocate. Listen with openness. Make an effort to put yourself in their shoes. Ask questions and be curious. Show empathy. Be the kind of audience that you want them to be for you.

When both partners are authentic and accountable—speaking up for

their wounds, sharing from their hearts, and listening to understand—
they develop the kind of emotional intimacy that we all long for. It can
be built only on a foundation of radical yet tactful honesty.

Create a Positive Feedback Loop

If your partner makes an effort to listen, give them lots of praise. Lots!
Even if you're not thrilled with their response, it's key to express gratitude for the effort. It's human nature to be motivated by hearing what
we're doing right and to be discouraged if all the feedback is negative.
How can you expect anyone to lean in eagerly if you're repeating over
and over again what they're getting wrong? They'll probably tune out
and stop trying.

What does work is praise for their effort, mirroring language that
creates safety, and opening up about your own experience. Your partner may not know how to do any of this yet. Remember, these are skills
that very few people learned from their families of origin. You're ex-
tending an invitation for them to meet you in a more authentic place.
If they're willing to make an effort, be patient as they learn and grow
with you.

If you're not getting back exactly what you hoped for, it doesn't
mean your partner doesn't care. It can certainly feel that way, but recognize it for what it is—something new and uncomfortable that they're
learning, too. Your partner is also a flawed human being with their
own attachment fears and inner child who has been hurt and wounded.
Give them the benefit of the doubt.

Your partner just needs to listen and try to understand. That *effort* is
the act of love. They don't need to get it all right, agree with you, or fill
a void inside you. You do that part for yourself. You're not reaching out
to be rescued by a magical fairy-tale character. You're an adult reaching
out to another adult you love for comfort, support, and connection.

They're there to be responsive to your needs in the same way you're there for them, but they're never responsible for *all* your emotional needs. Your Sage Self is the one who is always there to take care of you.

What to Do When Your Partner Disappoints You

How you speak up is crucial. But I'd be lying if I told you that the perfect words said the perfect way are guaranteed to work. Just as Monique and Ryan discovered, sometimes you communicate flawlessly and your partner still gets triggered. In that case, you'll have to take care of yourself until they're able to hear you—or make hard decisions about the relationship if they're never able to hear you.

When your partner reacts badly, it can make you feel as though your needs are too much. That's *never* true. But if you don't get a great response for any reason, it stings. When you take the time to show up like an adult and your partner's response is crap, it sucks and you may get triggered. But you have internal resources to help you cope with that. Here's what to do if you don't receive the response you want:

- Speak up no matter what
- Catch yourself and repair
- Self-soothe
- Filter feedback and express impact
- Discern how much to divulge
- Evaluate the relationship

What's Behind Your Partner's Response

If you speak up, even with all the skills you've learned in this book, you may still hurt your partner's feelings—not because you're doing anything wrong, but because they have wounds from the past just like you and are wired for an attachment sensitivity to anything you might say.

It's similar to what happens when you approach an injured animal. The predictable response is fear and confusion that manifests as aggression, even though you're trying to help. They may snarl and growl despite desperately needing you. The tricky thing is that your partner may also easily feel trapped, even when you're communicating clearly and maturely in an attempt to connect.

It may be difficult for you to express yourself without tripping the wires of their internal alarm system. Receiving even the most sensitively worded complaint is difficult; everyone's attachment radar is hypervigilant, and we're all prone to interpreting such disclosures as threats. As you'll recall from Chapter 2, the displeasure you express, even with something very small, can be coded by your partner's brain as a potential harbinger of abandonment and rejection.

When you approach your partner wanting to talk, they may detect a threat even if there isn't one. Their brain may churn a Negative Partner Story in which they're the bad guy. They may automatically assume they're being blamed, even when your language is gentle. In this case, you can reassure them that although you have something to share, you love them and they are good in your eyes.

Often when your partner hears that something has hurt you, they feel powerless and it's hard for them to manage. They may be uneasy about just sitting and listening without actually fixing your problem. Their automatic go-to may be to feel like they have to do something rather than just witnessing your feelings.

That's why it's so important to let them know: "There's no pressure for you to do anything in this moment. Could you just listen and try to understand? That makes me feel connected to you and helps so much."

Your reassurance may soothe and make it easier for them to hear that your specific complaint or need is not a condemnation of their global character.

Even with reassurance, it takes a certain degree of openness, ego strength, and emotional intelligence to absorb feedback. Perhaps your partner is high in narcissistic traits and struggles with empathy, or perhaps they simply haven't learned to be present for an emotional experience yet. If your partner isn't in touch with their own feelings at all, it will be difficult for them to show up for yours.

Maybe the most your partner can give isn't enough. Or maybe they're just at the beginning stage of their emotional development and can learn with you. You won't know until you start communicating differently. Then you can deal with whatever comes your way.

Speak Up No Matter What

Your decision to speak up can't be contingent on your partner's response. Regardless of your partner's limitations, you have to speak up. You have no control over what you get back, but you can ground yourself in the conviction that you're worthy of being heard.

Needing external approval puts you in a position of relinquishing your power. Of course it's natural to want your partner to respond well, but if you're reliant on that, then you'll be limited to speaking up only when you're certain of the outcome. A validating response is ideal, but you're communicating openly because it's best for you, not because it's palatable to your partner.

If you're taking responsibility for your side of the street and bringing your Sage Self to the conversation, you're doing your part. You're not responsible for how it lands. You can't live in a choke hold of conflict avoidance. You don't have to resort to avoidant behaviors at the first hint of discomfort. It's okay to disappoint or upset your partner as long as you're communicating responsibly and respectfully.

Catch Yourself and Repair

We know our limbic systems are primed for protective responses when we detect a threat to our relationship. This is simply because of how much our attachment bonds matter and how vital they are to our survival. It happens to all of us. You'll get triggered; your partner will get triggered. It won't go perfectly. Have grace for yourself; give grace to your partner. You can repair and move forward with a clean slate, and the more you do, the stronger your relationship becomes.

As you learned in Chapter 3, the goal is always to address, share, and repair, as Monique and Ryan did. Repair is what couples must do any time there's a disagreement, a misunderstanding, or any other small rupture. Fighting isn't the problem, but not repairing properly is. We don't stuff grievances inside and stew because that leads us down the road to disconnection. Instead, we repair and move on without resentment and animosity. Dr. John Gottman's research has shown that happy couples who stay together repair frequently and effectively.

Repair means owning your side of the street, taking responsibility for your contribution to the dynamic, and prioritizing connection over being right or winning. If you get a bad response from your partner and you're triggered, you may be tempted to resort to avoidant behavior yourself. It's okay—a small blip doesn't have to derail everything. Get yourself back on track by recalibrating, taking responsibility for your reaction, and offering a sincere apology.

Own your behavior regardless of what your partner does. Putting your ego aside to apologize demonstrates maturity and contributes to a win-win. Don't get hung up and convince yourself that your partner's poor response lets you off the hook. It's not tit for tat. Remind yourself that this relationship is important to you and your connection matters. Deep down, you have to care more about the long-term health of your relationship than about scoring a point in the moment.

There is no room for winning in relationships. If you want to make a case and prove you're right, be proclaimed the victor, triumph over your adversary, or die on the hill of egocentric pride, go to law school. If you're already an attorney, head on over to the courthouse. Those tactics have no place in a healthy relationship under any circumstances, ever. Ultimately taking accountability is freeing and empowering and feels good.

If you find yourself operating out of that mode, one of your protective parts has taken over with avoidant behavior. This may show up as getting defensive, explaining, blaming, pointing things out about your partner, or defending yourself and your honorable intentions.

Notice and validate that protective part in its effort to help you. Let that part know that you have better techniques now, such as speaking clearly and kindly about your feelings and needs. This is not the time to bring up or defend your intentions. No one wants to hear about that when their feelings are hurt.

Talk directly to the part of you that wants to protect you with avoidant behaviors. This inner conversation is a lifesaver in conflict and allows you to stay engaged and repair when needed. Sometimes all it takes is a quick correction in the moment. You know who you are; remind yourself. *I'm a good person and it's okay to make a mistake. I'm human and doing the best I can. I don't need to get upset if my partner is saying something I don't like. They're entitled to their feelings and experiences just as I am.*

If you feel yourself getting reactive:

- Pause and take a breath (or a longer time-out and pause if needed)
- Reconnect to your Sage Self
- Tell your partner what was happening inside you
- Apologize
- Start over

Jasmine and Camila Repair and Reconnect

Jasmine and Camila came into my office excited to report that they'd been able to pull off a repair on their own. The argument started when Camila made plans for the weekend without consulting Jasmine. Frequently in the past Jasmine reacted by suppressing her anger and self-silencing. But lately she was making an effort to speak up with Self-Connected Communication.

In this instance, Jasmine took a pause, processed her internal experience, and distilled it in her blueprint. She took care to approach Camila gently by Taking a Delicate Dive. Despite a good start, Camila got triggered and became defensive when Jasmine shared her frustration. Camila's defensive response then triggered Jasmine.

"You never listen to me. You always get defensive. I'm so over it," Jasmine exclaimed.

But she caught herself raising her voice, blaming, and using absolutes, so she stopped and recalibrated.

Jasmine took a breath and said, "Wait, I'm sorry I got heated. I was feeling anxious and stressed. A part of me started to raise my voice. I was blaming you, and that's not right. I would like to share my true feelings and concerns, and I'm open and willing to listen to yours, too. Can we start over?"

Camila was able to receive Jasmine's in-the-moment repair. She took a breath. "I'm sorry, too. I got triggered as well. I'm not even sure why yet, but I was definitely getting defensive. You don't deserve that. Let's try again and take turns really listening to each other. I want us both to feel heard."

Taking accountability and offering a clean, authentic apology defuses mounting tension. Sometimes I get feisty with my husband when I'm upset, but with awareness and connection to myself, I often catch it and repair by saying something like "I'm sorry I was raising my voice. A part of me was getting activated. Let me start over and try this differently."

This resets my nervous system and reconnects me to my Sage Self. It also lets my husband hear that I'm willing to own my behavior.

Just like Jasmine and Camila, you can reject escalating with avoidant behaviors and choose to repair and reconnect. Your mindful awareness and willingness to take responsibility for your all-too-human reaction is often all it takes to get back on track. You'll have a very different and much more connected outcome when you choose this path.

Remember that nothing good happens in communication when your nervous system isn't regulated. If you need more than a breath or two, call a time-out and come back after a pause when you're fully reconnected to your Sage Self. You must assess yourself, discern what you need in the moment, and be flexible accordingly.

Self-Soothe After a Partner's Disappointing Response

Even if you don't get reactive, you may find yourself disappointed by your partner's response and in need of some good inner-child self-soothing. This is the time to offer the little girl inside validation and self-compassion—to really be with her, comfort her, and let her know that her needs matter.

You can be disappointed in your partner's reaction yet not fall apart. Be proud of yourself for stepping into the unknown with your truth. Praise yourself for your courage and willingness to let yourself be seen and known. You had the guts to risk putting yourself out there in your quest for emotional intimacy. You didn't want to end up feeling empty and fossilized with resentment and did everything in your power to come from a kind, respectful adult place.

If your partner can't show up, that hurts, but you'll be okay. That's on them. You can still be connected to yourself inside even when you can't be connected to your partner. You'll draw your power and worthiness from the connection between your Sage Self and your inner child.

Sometimes self-soothing is as simple as talking to your inner child. This helps you shift into observational awareness, harnessing your higher-functioning brain to bring yourself into regulation.

Remind the little girl that this is not the past, it's the present, and you're here with her now. She doesn't have to be part of adult interactions. You can protect her. Your Sage Self is capable of handling it. Her needs matter, and you can meet them even when your partner can't or won't. There is a loving grown-up here with that little one now, and that's you.

Self-Soothing Mantras

A great way to self-soothe is by reciting an internal mantra. When it's challenging to stay calm in the face of your partner's reaction, this can help you stay grounded and present.

My favorite mantra is a riff I've adapted from psychologist Ellyn Bader's developmental model of couples therapy. When I'm feeling the protective urge to react poorly, I repeat to myself:

My partner's reaction to me is their problem, not mine.
It's about them, not me.
I do not need to get so upset.
I do not need to own this problem.
I only need to listen and try to understand.
If it crosses a line I'm uncomfortable with, I will remove myself.
I will take care of me no matter what.

Remember that you always have control of your external reaction. Your alarm bells may go off if you sense a threat, but it's usually not the emergency your first instinct suggests. Regardless, you can manage your reaction. As an adult you can handle your partner being disappointed or upset with you and listen to their experience with curiosity.

Take Feedback from Your Partner

If your partner offers feedback, be the kind of listener you long for. Be open to hearing a narrative different from the Negative Partner Story your mind generated in a triggered moment. When they tell you what they're thinking and feeling, believe them. Your Negative Partner Story isn't their truth. They can't speak for your inner world, and you can't speak for theirs. Don't assume. No matter how well you think you know them, you'll most likely be wrong about their intentions and get into a dead-end loop of avoidant behavior that leaves both of you feeling awful with nothing resolved.

There's no better way to get into an argument than to make assumptions about your partner and throw them out there as if they're absolute truths.

Take a break if you need it. Validate your partner's experience if they share it with you. You don't have to agree with them. You're respecting their right to their experience and their subjective interpretation. Don't take it so personally. Just as your stuff is about you, their stuff is about them.

It's also important to filter your partner's feedback and choose what you absorb. Maybe they have some good points that you can learn from. Maybe what they're saying about you doesn't fit at all and should be dismissed.

Remember that your partner's reaction says more about them—their wounds, their protection, their own emotional development—and much less about you and the relationship. Listen to your intuition. Don't accept everything you hear. If your partner tells you that you're ridiculous for feeling the way you do, check in with your Sage Self. That part of you always knows what's true. No one defines your reality but you.

Let your partner know how their response impacts you. No matter what, you can express your experience and stand powerfully in your truth. Simply share what's happening inside.

You can say something like, "This is me reaching out to connect with you. Our relationship is really important to me. When you get defensive, it hurts and makes me feel lonely. The story in my mind is that I can't tell you anything. In order to feel connected to you and safer about sharing my feelings, I need you to listen without getting defensive. You don't have to agree with me; just try to understand. I want to share things so we can be closer. Are you willing to work on this with me?"

This is a clear statement of the impact they had on you and an invitation to connect. The question at the end is intended to elicit a response. Your partner is either buying in or bowing out.

Discern How Much to Divulge

You also don't have to make yourself utterly vulnerable until you're sure your partner is receptive. Gauge their reactions as you self-disclose. Discern how much you're willing to share. There's a difference between working through a little fear and discomfort to take a risk that can generate connection and laying yourself completely bare when your partner repeatedly shows that they cannot or will not receive what you're offering. You're not going to open up with everything you distilled in your blueprint if your partner continues to be dismissive or defensive or shuts down.

You don't want to throw your little girl with all of her greatest vulnerabilities out there if you know your partner won't be tender with her. That's not fair. It will only reinjure your inner child and build distrust between her and you. Your Sage Self can handle it if your partner responds poorly, but the little girl inside you should never have to. By connecting to your Sage Self—your intuition, your internal compass—you can discern whether it's safe to go deeper. That's good stewardship. You show up like an adult, do your part, and make decisions based on what you receive.

Evaluate the Relationship

If you're consistently clear in addressing your concerns but unable to have safe, connected conversations, evaluating the relationship offers vital information about its limitations. It may be painful to contend with, but this information empowers you to make informed choices about your future.

Sometimes relationships need to end. You have only one short, beautiful life to live, and you have a right to enjoy it. If your relationship isn't giving you what you need, you'll have built your self-esteem back up to the point where you can make decisions based on what you know you deserve: love and respect. Though that won't be easy, it's better than a lifetime in the cave of resentment.

Don't settle.

Only you can decide what that means. There are many unique variables to be considered. Deciding to stay or go is a complex decision that relies on a multitude of sensitive factors. For some, this includes financial restrictions, concerns about children, social shame, and religious barriers. For most, there's the dread of facing the unavoidable heartbreak that comes with dissolving an attachment bond, no matter how flawed or unfulfilling the relationship has become.

This is a highly subjective decision that comes from listening to your own voice and intuition. The following questions may help you evaluate exactly where you stand.

- *Is this relationship worth working through?*
- *Can we repair and move forward?*
- *Have I truly done all I can do?*
- *Am I showing up like an emotionally mature partner?*
- *What is my greatest fear about ending the relationship?*
- *What is my greatest fear about staying in the relationship?*
- *What logistical obstacles are there to ending the relationship?*
- *Are these obstacles holding me back from what I really want?*

At this point if you're not sure what decision to make, you may want to work with a therapist. For help finding a therapist, see the resources at the back of the book.

Don't rush yourself; it's a difficult process and a very personal decision. But understand that whatever you decide, you're going to be fine.

When you take the risk to put yourself out there and don't get the response you're hoping for, it's hurtful and disappointing but survivable. You have tools to self-soothe, filter feedback, and establish boundaries. You can maintain an adult standard of communication by staying connected to your Sage Self. The stronger your connection to this part of you, the more your confidence grows and the less your well-being depends on your partner's reaction. If you're doing your part with Self-

Connected Communication, you'll see your relationship more clearly and be able to make adult decisions about whether to stay or go, based on your partner's willingness and capacity. No matter what, you've found your voice and learned how to use it. The foundation is in place. In the next chapter we'll dive into building the habit of speaking up, so no matter what relationship you're in, you're comfortable using your voice for the rest of your life.

Questions for Reflection

- Do you notice a change in your partner's response when you practice Self-Connected Communication? Does your vulnerability seem to soften them?
- What might your little-girl part need to hear from you to self-soothe when your partner doesn't react well?
- Do you notice when your partner is making an effort to listen? Do you tend to praise them for this? Or are you often critical of how they respond to you?
- How do you normally initiate a repair? What language might you use the next time you get triggered and don't react well to get the conversation back on track?
- Have you ever contemplated ending your relationship? If so, what role do you believe you play in what's not working? Do you truly feel that you've done all you can do?

CHAPTER 9

Building the Habit of Speaking Up

Olivia had spent a lifetime holding her feelings in, and she had come to therapy on her own to find and use her voice. Jack didn't think they needed therapy—he didn't feel like they had time, and he didn't understand what they'd get out of it, anyway. They rarely argued; things were pretty good in his view.

But Oliva harbored dissatisfactions Jack didn't know about. He wasn't initiating sex as much as he used to, often seeming distracted and disengaged. In the evenings after work, he sat in front of the TV scrolling on his phone, or went out to the back porch to have a drink and a cigar while she was inside managing dinner, the kids' homework, and bedtime solo.

Before she learned Self-Connected Communication, Olivia's typical pattern was to doubt and dismiss her own feelings. She'd jump from thinking, *I want to throttle you, Jack,* to *Maybe I'm overreacting?* Then she'd tell herself it wasn't that big a deal and definitely not worth a fight. She feared coming across as a nag. *If I'm still upset about it twenty-four hours later, then I'll say something*, she would reason. But by the next day she usually got busy and forgot. Until the next time. Each time she suppressed her feelings, the frustration and resentment grew . . . until she inevitably blew up at him over some seemingly insignificant thing. After Olivia calmed down, she was mortified by her outburst, but she had never gotten to the root cause of her avoidant behavior. The result of all of this: She and Jack had grown more distant and disconnected over time.

After working with me regularly, Olivia found her voice and learned to use it. She wanted a few things out of her relationship with Jack—specifically, a more engaged partnership and a more active sex life. So she started telling him this. She shared with Jack that she felt lonely when he disconnected in the evenings, and that their dwindling sex life made her feel insecure and question his attraction to her.

To her pleasant surprise, Jack was sympathetic when she approached him clearly and vulnerably using Self-Connected Communication. He explained that he was so stressed and overworked that he had simply shut down lately. He had no idea she felt rejected and found her just as beautiful as ever. Sometimes Jack assumed *she* didn't want to have sex because she never initiated. He figured she wanted to be left alone. This huge, unspoken misunderstanding about their sex life had been generated by their lack of communication. Now they had shifted it from an unspeakable issue to a solvable problem. They *both* wanted to reignite their sexual connection, and there were actionable steps they would take to make it happen.

With this success under her belt, Olivia was feeling more self-assured and connected to Jack. Now she was working on building a habit of speaking up in other parts of her life, so she could continue to communicate this way in her marriage, but also with her friendships, with her parents, and in her community.

Olivia knows she has to make speaking up a habit by practicing all the time; it's still hard, and she's still human. She has made a commitment to exercising her newfound voice daily so this brand-new muscle doesn't atrophy. She's determined to keep her communication muscles strong.

It's not enough to find and use your voice on occasion; you have to exercise your empowered voice daily. Luckily, there are ways you can keep this momentum going in all aspects of your life. Fear and anxiety often pop up in the face of conflict, tempting you to slide back into avoidant behavior. But with the following regular practices, you can hold yourself accountable to continue speaking up and keep your voice primed for healthy communication.

Practice Mindfulness

Cultivating a habit of using your voice relies on a bedrock of inner awareness. But let's be honest, most of us rarely stop to connect with our inner worlds. We're accustomed to paying attention to external stimuli, distracting ourselves with a text, a snack, or a news headline whenever difficult emotions arise. Particularly in this age of nonstop technology, it's easier than ever to ping from one thing to another all day, every day, with little to no awareness of what's happening in your body. To exercise your voice and keep it strong, you'll need to tune in to your inner world on a daily basis and strengthen your observing ego. One of the best ways to do this is through mindfulness.

The ability to become aware of what your brain and nervous system are telling you is known as the *observing ego*. Your observing ego allows you to step outside yourself to perceive your actions, as well as any defenses and motivations behind those actions, and (crucially) also determine the effect those actions may be having on the person you're interacting with. It's a powerful ability, and when you connect to your Sage Self, you bring your observing ego online. This is the part of you that has conscious awareness of what's happening as it's happening. It also conditions your ability to relate to yourself.

The human mind is designed to run amok. Some of us have busier brains than others, but we're all subject to "monkey mind" from time to time. This means our minds wander, jumping from thought to thought, coming up with all sorts of random ideas, tangents, and wonderings, like monkeys swinging from branch to branch. One minute we're laser focused on finishing a presentation, but the next we're revisiting the time we got lost on vacation and found the best little bistro off the beaten path. Or we're driving to work and get so lost in daydreaming about our to-do list that we don't even remember getting off the highway.

In their 2010 article "A Wandering Mind Is an Unhappy Mind" in *Science*, Harvard psychologists Matthew A. Killingsworth and Daniel T. Gilbert reported their research findings that our minds wanders for 46.9 percent of our waking hours. This means we're not focused on what we're doing and we're off in La-La Land, reminiscing or fretting over the past, planning or preparing for the future. While mental meandering is perfectly normal, they determined that we're much happier when we're more fully present.

Our minds may swing from the branches of our thoughts like monkeys in the rainforest, but we're not at the mercy of the brain's tendency to wander. When we practice mindfulness, we can gently bring ourselves back to the present. This creates new neural pathways for being more self-aware, engaged, and intentional.

Your inside world is as rich with color and texture as the most beautiful vista in nature. By closing your eyes, getting still, and going inward with curiosity, you can connect with your full experience and different parts of yourself, which is crucial to communicating effectively.

Being present and observing these inner sensations is known as mindfulness. Based on a secularized version of Buddhist principles, mindfulness is the practice of cultivating a nonjudgmental awareness of the present moment. In 1979 at the University of Massachusetts Medical School, Dr. Jon Kabat-Zinn developed a program called Mindfulness-Based Stress Reduction (MBSR) that pioneered the practice and set its popularization in motion. He originally designed the program to help patients adjust to their stress and pain, finding that it vastly improved their ability to deal with what was outside their control. Over time mindfulness has been applied to coping with situations such as illness and mental health issues, including depression and anxiety, as well as being a simple daily practice for a more fully embodied way of being.

Mindfulness is instrumental in taking care of yourself emotionally and in communicating effectively with your partner. It gives you the ability to know your inner world and advocate for what you want and need. Without it, we're at the mercy of reactionary impulses generated by lurking attachment fears and transient feelings.

It is a simple but powerful tool for being fully present and aware of whatever is happening. When you're practicing mindfulness, you tune in to the present moment, bring a gentle awareness, and refrain from judgment, accepting the experience as it occurs.

MINDFUL BREATHING

Read through the following, then set a timer for three minutes, and begin as directed:

- Close your eyes, take three deep breaths, and get settled.

- Notice your feet on the floor, your body in your chair, and the air against your skin.

- Follow your breath from the inhale all the way down into your lungs.

- You can imagine a balloon in your stomach that inflates as you breathe in and deflates as you breathe out. This will help you track your breath as you go.

- You may notice thoughts popping up to distract you. That's perfectly fine and completely normal—it's what your brain is wired for. Don't judge yourself for your thoughts or feelings. Simply bring your attention back to the breath, tracking and noticing it until the timer runs out.

There is no right or wrong, just reflect and make note of your observations:

- What was this mindful breathing exercise like for you?

- Did you find it easy to stay with your breath?

- Did you become distracted?

- What kind of thoughts did you have?

- Did you notice any body sensations or feelings?

We are not our thoughts; we are complex beings composed of many parts of self, with varied neural impulses—including feelings, thoughts, sensations, and urges. We can observe our thoughts and experience our feelings as they occur without getting hijacked by them. By becoming more conscious, we have more separation and space from what we're thinking and feeling, and we can self-soothe, recognize when we need a pause, and choose how we express ourselves to our partners.

Consistent, effective communication is almost impossible without the ability to witness your experience.

If you don't already have a mindfulness practice, I highly recommend developing one. Even five to ten minutes a day can create new neural pathways for self-awareness and consciousness that will support you in communicating intentionally. A regular mindfulness practice also enhances happiness and well-being. On the relationship front, it helps you notice when you're avoiding conflict—when you're tempted to dismiss something that stirs inside you before you've explored its significance.

Journal Moments of Avoidance

Another great way to build a habit of speaking up is to journal about the small moments of potential conflict that arise each day. It's important to track and assess your progress as you go. Noticing, reflecting, and evaluating your progress is the best way to condition your voice and continue to improve. Keeping a regular log will help you see your own patterns of avoidance and work to break them in the future. Take a few moments to jot down any time you resort to avoidant behaviors, or have the urge to do so.

As you reflect on what happened in the instances in which you didn't speak up, answer the following questions:

- *Why did I avoid communicating in this instance?*
- *What did I tell myself to rationalize or justify the choice to stay quiet?*
- *What could I have said, had I decided to speak up?*

Also write down any of the instances in which you did speak up, and then answer the following questions:

- *What was the hardest part about using my voice in this instance?*
- *Did it feel less scary to speak up than I thought it would?*

- *What did I say to myself that made it easier to use my voice?*
- *Looking back, is there anything I could have said or done differently?*

Answering these questions will help you strengthen your speaking-up muscles. The more reinforcement, awareness, and practice, the better. This also gives you a chance to learn from your mistakes and continue to improve.

Be gentle and curious with yourself. Accept whatever happened without judgment, and see your experiences as continued opportunities for growth.

This business of being human means we're not gonna get it right much of the time. As you've learned, we're wired to avoid pain and discomfort and protect our connections. Therefore, confronting issues by speaking up often feels counterintuitive and scary. But the willingness to consistently act in the face of that fear, make mistakes, and learn from them is the only way we grow.

Progress is messy, nonlinear, and never perfect. It's two steps forward and four back; then five steps forward and three back. Growing necessitates getting out of your comfort zone and wading around in the muck, again and again each day, even when it doesn't feel very good and the long-term benefits are elusive. But once you embrace the reality of trial and error and commit to it consistently, your evolution as an emotionally mature communicator will explode.

Address Small Conflicts Quickly

Through mindfulness and journaling, you'll notice those small moments of conflict when you succumb to avoidance. This is an opportunity to push yourself to address even minor things that bother you—the tiny blips of annoyance that offer you a chance to practice speaking up. Don't sweep little things under the rug. Challenge yourself to address the daily small stuff with Self-Connected Communication.

Here's an example of addressing small conflicts quickly that Olivia shared with me in session:

Olivia and Jack were going to a dinner party with his friends from work. Olivia had bought a new dress for the occasion that showed off all the weight training she'd been doing recently. It was a little more form-fitting than what she usually wore, but she loved how confident and sexy the dress made her feel. As they were getting ready, Jack turned to her and remarked, "You're wearing *that*?" The expression on his face seemed like disgust. Olivia deflated. *He doesn't think I look good. Maybe I'm delusional and this dress looks terrible*, she thought. A protective part of her wanted to protest by firing back: *Why would you say that to me? That's so rude!* She had an even stronger urge to bypass the remark, change her outfit, and pretend the whole thing never happened.

But Olivia had been practicing mindfulness and journaling regularly about such moments and noticed her thoughts and the urge to sweep the matter under the rug. She checked herself and found that while she was irritated and hurt by what seemed like an insensitive remark at best, she wasn't triggered. She didn't need to take a pause, but she did need to speak up and address her feelings directly.

She took a couple of deep breaths to access her Sage Self and speak up about her feelings clearly and kindly:

"I'm sure you didn't intend to hurt me, but I was feeling so good about how I looked in this dress and so excited to wear it that when you said, 'Are you wearing that?' it really hurt my feelings. The story in my mind was that you don't think I look good. Can you help me understand what you meant by that comment?"

Olivia empowered herself to be vulnerable in the moment and take the risk to let him know she was hurt. She held on to her adult self and got curious instead of reacting with avoidant behavior. Olivia was open to hearing where Jack's comment was coming from, rather than assuming her Negative Partner Story was true.

"No, not at all. My comment was about the fact that I didn't think we were getting so dressed up. You look *incredible* in that dress! You're so hot I wish we didn't even have to go to dinner." Jack grinned and gave her a kiss.

Olivia felt a wave of relief come over her. It was obvious it had been a misunderstanding, and she felt even better about the fact that she had said something. It would have been so easy to sweep this under the rug, but then she would have missed an opportunity to exercise her voice. By being willing to confront the moment head on, Olivia defused the tension, resolved her hurt feelings, and stayed connected to Jack.

Little moments like these can add up to accumulated frustration, Negative Partner Stories, and even resentment when the air isn't cleared. Push yourself to practice speaking up with your partner at every opportunity. This is a crucial part of habit formation—seizing upon something small. Most people make the mistake of trying to make changes that are too big instead of focusing on making small realistic changes consistently. In fact, the smaller the action, the better. Practice using your voice.

Here are some simple steps to remember for these little moments when you're not triggered but need to flex and use your speaking-up muscle:

1. Take a few deep breaths before speaking up.
2. Start with a positive, if possible.
3. Use "I" statements to express your feelings.
4. Ask for what you need.

All of your feelings are important, and it's key that you identify when you're feeling resentment and name it with your partner.

As you push yourself to vocalize these small everyday irritations, you'll notice a surprising benefit. Not only does speaking up become more of a habit and get easier, but ironically the more you communicate about the small things as they happen, the less you have to communicate about your relationship overall. Let this be the motivation that guides you.

Schedule Weekly Check-Ins

I encourage couples to commit to weekly check-ins. Based on Dr. John Gottman's concept of having "State of the Union" meetings, this is a great way to make sure you don't sweep things under the rug! Schedule a weekly check-in with your partner to reflect on your relationship, share positive feedback, and address conflict from a nonreactive state. These meetings deepen intimacy, provide fertile ground for exercising your voice, address conflict proactively, and prevent unnecessary reactive and destructive conflict.

Set aside thirty minutes or so once a week for an uninterrupted, device-free conversation in a comfortable spot in your home. Take turns sharing and receiving without giving advice or problem-solving. This is the time to practice curiosity, active listening, empathy, and validation as you share and receive.

1. **Start by expressing something you appreciated about your partner this week.** Be specific. It can be something very small as long as it's authentic. Don't skip this important step in letting your partner hear what they're getting right.

2. **Select an issue to process from the week and take turns sharing and listening.** Perhaps it's something small that you avoided and journaled about later. Now is the time to tell your partner about it in clear, kind language. Be mindful of your tone. Focus on your own feelings, use "I" statements, and ask for what you need going forward. Challenge yourself to be self-focused. Nobody takes feedback well when they feel criticized, blamed, accused, attacked, or at fault (even if you think your partner is at fault!). Instead, take responsibility and own your experience. For example, you could say something like, "When you told me that you didn't want to go to the party, something happened for me, and I want to tell you about my experience. I felt frustrated. Underneath that frustration were hurt and loneliness. This party is really important to me. I get a message that you don't care. It would mean so much to me if you'd reconsider."

3. **When you're the listener, stay curious and open.** Show your engagement by nodding, asking clarifying questions, and repeating back what you're hearing to make sure you're getting it right. This lets your partner know you're with them and that you care about what they have to say. If you notice yourself getting triggered, slow down and breathe. Remind yourself that this is your partner's experience and it's about them, not you. If you need a break, take a pause and come back to the meeting and the topic when you're regulated.

4. **Offer genuine praise to each other for your efforts to listen.** It's not easy to hear feedback, and you both deserve recognition for trying. Be generous with praise and give yourselves a pat on the back for working together as a team.

Weekly check-ins are the antithesis of avoidant behavior. By practicing regularly, you're both exercising your voices and keeping your skills sharp. You're also ensuring that small issues get resolved and don't fester. If I could give one piece of advice on building relationship habits to every newlywed couple, it would be this. Make weekly check-ins a habit at the beginning of your relationship. You'll build a scaffolding for addressing issues regularly and effectively, and you'll have fewer arguments. This is such a healthy, productive way to repair as you go. This kind of engagement builds closeness and understanding, deepens intimacy, and addresses conflict constructively—before it hardens into resentment and disconnection.

Your Voice Is Your Power

The cost of avoiding conflict is too great to bear: Resentment corrodes your well-being and creates a disconnected relationship that either dissolves or trudges along on life support. With Self-Connected Communication you can address conflict, harness it for growth, and have the kind of relationship you deserve—with yourself and your partner.

When you share the truth about what's going on inside you, you're being an emotionally mature, authentic partner. You're taking responsibility for your part and what you can control. But remember, the most important thing is that you're taking care of yourself.

I've walked this road in my own life and will continue to be on this journey right alongside you. As a reformed people-pleaser who was chronically terrified of rocking the boat and had no clue how to express my needs, I've learned how to speak up for myself in healthy ways that help me get heard.

Your voice is your power. When you realize that power is within you and you've had it all along, you're free. Instead of betraying yourself, make the choice to honor yourself by speaking up.

I can't promise you'll save your relationship, but I do know you'll save yourself.

Questions for Reflection

- What practice will be most useful to you in making speaking up a habit?
- What are your biggest takeaways from this book?
- How has your perspective on avoiding conflict changed?
- Are you ready to live your best life by speaking up for yourself?
- Are you feeling excited and hopeful about what lies ahead?

Clinical Background and
Resources for Finding a Therapist

⸻

I've developed the Self-Connected Communication model from my clinical work using attachment science and evidence-based therapies such as Emotionally Focused Therapy, Intimacy from the Inside Out, Internal Family Systems, the Gottman Method of couples therapy, the developmental model of couples therapy, ego state therapy, Mindfulness-Based Stress Reduction, and cognitive behavioral therapy.

While multiple approaches have informed my process, I am certified in Emotionally Focused Therapy (EFT), the gold standard in evidence-based treatment for couples, and Eye Movement Desensitization and Reprocessing (EMDR), a transformative therapy for the treatment of trauma, post-traumatic stress disorder (PTSD), and a host of other presenting concerns. If you're interested in learning more about any of these therapeutic modalities, I've included a list of recommended reading at the end of the book, as well as resources for finding a therapist.

Practicing for years with these experiential therapies has given me a profound understanding of the power of the subconscious mind and how having an embodied connection leads to growth. I've witnessed and experienced how we heal and thrive through connection with ourselves and our closest loved ones. I've seen the evidence of neuroplasticity—that the brain changes with conscious awareness and each little choice to behave differently.

If you're looking for a therapist, here are a few good places to start:

- Psychology Today (https://www.psychologytoday.com/us) is one of the best online directories to find a therapist in your area.
- If you wish to use insurance, contact your insurance company and ask for a list of covered providers.
- For quality low- or no-cost services, contact your local colleges or universities. Many have counseling clinics where trained graduate students offer free, supervised sessions.
- If you're seeking relationship therapy, make sure to select a provider with extensive training and experience in treating couples.

Other Mental Health Resources

- National Domestic Violence Hotline: 800-799-7233
- Suicide and Crisis Lifeline: 988

Acknowledgments

This book was born from both hardship and healing—like so many of the most valuable lessons. As I worked with clients and heard them voice the very same words I once said to myself in moments when I failed to speak up, I knew I had to write this book. I'm grateful for the difficult times that have shaped me and led me here to be able to help others.

With great gratitude, I want to thank my agent, Bonnie Solow, for taking a chance on me, believing in my message, and helping to bring this dream to life. You are a one of a kind! To my editors, Michelle Howry and Ashley Di Dio—thank you for your kindness, expertise, and dedication. You are incredibly talented and made the daunting process of writing a book feel manageable. Your willingness to listen and truly understand my vision has meant everything. I am forever grateful to the incredible team at Penguin Random House for ushering this book into the world.

I also owe a debt of gratitude to the many teachers and thought leaders who have shaped my understanding of relationships—Alfred Adler, Sue Johnson, John Gottman, Stan Tatkin, Esther Perel, Liz Phillips, and so many others. Your work has challenged and inspired me, pushing me to stretch and deepen my practice.

ACKNOWLEDGMENTS

To my clients—you have taught me more than I could have ever learned in school or training. Thank you for sharing your stories, for your trust, and for allowing me to walk alongside you on your beautiful journeys.

To those who have lifted me up along the way: the many dear friends who stood by me, celebrated my wins, and held space for me in my moments of doubt, thank you! The best life is one where friendships like ours exist, and I feel deeply fortunate. Anna Vatuone and Laura Belotti—your tutelage, tactical guidance, and emotional support has been invaluable.

And finally but most important, to my family—thank you for your love, encouragement, and unwavering belief in me. Mom, this book would not have come together without your patient listening and hours of unpaid editing. Dad, thank you for offering your insights as a man from another generation who has had to sit through far more "emotional stuff" than you probably ever imagined. I am who I am, in all my glory, because of you both. To my husband—thank you for encouraging me to write this book and for supporting me through every step along the way. You have been my sounding board, my steadfast believer, and my most patient guinea pig for testing out "therapy stuff" over the years. To Charlotte and Curran, you are my raison d'être—thank you for the gift of being your mom.

Recommended Reading

Atlas of the Heart: Mapping Meaningful Connection and the Language of Human Experience by Brené Brown, PhD, MSW

Buddha's Brain: The Practical Neuroscience of Happiness, Love & Wisdom by Rick Hanson, PhD, with Richard Mendius, MD

Feel the Fear . . . and Do It Anyway: Dynamic Techniques for Turning Fear, Indecision, and Anger into Power, Action, and Love by Susan Jeffers, PhD

Hold Me Tight: Seven Conversations for a Lifetime of Love by Dr. Sue Johnson

Mindfulness: An Eight-Week Plan for Finding Peace in a Frantic World by Mark Williams and Danny Penman

No Bad Parts: Healing Trauma & Restoring Wholeness with the Internal Family Systems Model by Richard C. Schwartz, PhD

The Relationship Cure: A Five-Step Guide to Strengthening Your Marriage, Family, and Friendships by John M. Gottman, PhD, and Joan DeClaire

Self-Compassion: The Proven Power of Being Kind to Yourself by Kristin Neff, PhD

The State of Affairs: Rethinking Infidelity by Esther Perel

The Relationship Cure: The Five-Step Guide to Strengthening Your Marriage, Family, and Friendships by John M. Gottman, PhD, and Joan DeClaire

Us: Getting Past You & Me to Build a More Loving Relationship by Terrence Real

Wired for Love: How Understanding Your Partner's Brain and Attachment Style Can Help You Defuse Conflict and Build a Secure Relationship by Stan Tatkin, PsyD

You Are the One You've Been Waiting For: Applying Internal Family Systems to Intimate Relationships by Richard C. Schwartz, PhD

Bibliography

Anderson, Frank G., Martha Sweezy, and Richard C. Schwartz. *Internal Family Systems Skills Training Manual: Trauma-Informed Treatment for Anxiety, Depression, PTSD & Substance Abuse.* PESI Publishing & Media, 2017.

Brown, Brené. *Rising Strong: How the Ability to Reset Transforms the Way We Live, Love, Parent, and Lead.* Random House, 2015.

Campbell, Susan, and John Grey. *Five-Minute Relationship Repair: Quickly Heal Upsets, Deepen Intimacy, and Use Differences to Strengthen Love.* New World Library, 2015.

Dweck, Carol S. *Mindset: The New Psychology of Success.* Ballantine Books, 2008.

Forsyth, John P., and Georg H. Eifert. *The Mindfulness & Acceptance Workbook for Anxiety: A Guide to Breaking Free from Anxiety, Phobias & Worry Using Acceptance & Commitment Therapy,* third edition. New Harbinger, 2025.

Fosha, Diana, Daniel J. Siegel, and Marion F. Solomon, eds. *The Healing Power of Emotion: Affective Neuroscience, Development & Clinical Practice.* Norton, 2009.

Goewey, Don Joseph. *The End of Stress: Four Steps to Rewire Your Brain*. Atria, 2014.

Gottman, John M., and Joan DeClaire. *The Relationship Cure: A 5 Step Guide to Strengthening Your Marriage, Family, and Friendships*. Harmony Books, 2002.

Gottman, John M., and Nan Silver. *The Seven Principles for Making Marriage Work: A Practical Guide from the Country's Foremost Relationship Expert*. Harmony Books, 1999.

Harris, Russ. *ACT Made Simple: An Easy-to-Read Primer on Acceptance and Commitment Therapy*. New Harbinger, 2019.

Herbine-Blank, Toni, and Martha Sweezy. *Internal Family Systems Couple Therapy Skills Manual: Healing Relationships with Intimacy from the Inside Out*. PESI Publishing & Media, 2021.

Herbine-Blank, Toni, Donna M. Kerpelman, and Martha Sweezy, *Intimacy from the Inside Out: Courage and Compassion in Couple Therapy*. Routledge, 2016.

Johnson, Susan M. *Attachment Theory in Practice: Emotionally Focused Therapy (EFT) with Individuals, Couples, and Families*. Guilford Press, 2019.

———. *Hold Me Tight: Seven Conversations for a Lifetime of Love*. Little, Brown Spark, 2008.

———. *The Practice of Emotionally Focused Couple Therapy: Creating Connection*, 2nd ed. Brunner-Routledge, 2004.

Kabat-Zinn, Jon. *Full Catastrophe Living: Using the Wisdom of Your Body and Mind to Face Stress, Pain, and Illness, Fifteenth Anniversary Edition*. Random House, 2005.

———. *Wherever You Go, There You Are: Mindfulness Meditation in Everyday Life, Tenth Anniversary Edition*. Hyperion eBooks, 2005.

Lisle, Douglas J., and Alan Goldhamer. *The Pleasure Trap: Mastering the Hidden Force That Undermines Health & Happiness*. Healthy Living, 2003.

Mikulincer, Mario, and Phillip R. Shaver. *Attachment Theory Expanded: Security Dynamics in Individuals, Dyads, Groups, and Societies*. Guilford Press, 2023.

Neff, Kristin. *Self-Compassion: The Proven Power of Being Kind to Yourself*. William Morrow, 2011.

Porges, Stephen W. *The Polyvagal Theory: Neurophysiological Foundations of Emotions, Attachment, Communication, and Self-Regulation*.
Norton, 2011.

Real, Terrence. *Us: Getting Past You & Me to Build a More Loving Relationship*. Rodale Books, 2022.

Riess, Helen. *The Empathy Effect: Seven Neuroscience-Based Keys for Transforming the Way We Live, Love, Work, and Connect Across Differences*. Sounds True, 2018.

Schwartz, Richard C. *You Are the One You've Been Waiting For: Applying Internal Family Systems to Intimate Relationships*. Sounds True, 2023.

Shapiro, Robin. *Easy Ego State Interventions: Strategies for Working with Parts*. Norton, 2016.

Siegel, Daniel J. *The Developing Mind: How Relationships and the Brain Interact to Shape Who We Are*, 3rd ed. Guilford Press, 2020.

Taylor, Jill Bolte. *Whole Brain Living: The Anatomy of Choice and the Four Characters That Drive Our Life*. Hay House, 2021.

Index

Photo © Kristia Knowles Photography

Colette Jane Fehr is a licensed psychotherapist specializing in couples therapy. Her expert advice has been featured in *The New York Times*, *The Wall Street Journal*, *Oprah Daily*, and on television and radio stations nationwide. She gave a popular TEDx Talk, "Secrets of a Couples Therapist: How to Find What's Missing in Your Relationship Before It's Too Late," at USFSM in Sarasota, Florida. Colette also cohosts *Insights from the Couch: Mental Health at Midlife*, a podcast dedicated to helping women navigate midlife with clarity and confidence. A native New Yorker, Colette now lives in Orlando, Florida, with her husband and is the proud mother of two adult daughters.

Visit Colette Fehr Online

colettejanefehr.com
☉ ColetteJaneFehr